WRITER-FILES

General Editor: Simon Trussler

Associate Editor: Malcolm Page

File on
NICHOLS

Compiled by Andrew Parkin

Methuen Drama

A Methuen Drama Book
First published in 1993 as a paperback original by
Methuen Drama

Copyright in the compilation
©1993 by Andrew Parkin
Copyright in the series format
©1993 by Methuen Drama
Copyright in the editorial presentation
©1993 by Simon Trussler

Typeset in 9/10 Times by
L. Anderson Typesetting,
Woodchurch, Kent TN26 3TB

ISBN 0-413-65600-1

British Library Cataloguing in Publication Data
is available from the British Library

Front cover photograph of Peter Nichols
by Tom Miller

Contents

The theatre is, by its nature, an ephemeral art: yet it is a daunting task to track down the newspaper reviews, or contemporary statements from the writer or his director, which are often all that remain to help us recreate some sense of what a particular production was like. This series is therefore intended to make readily available a selection of the comments that the critics made about the plays of leading modern dramatists at the time of their production — and to trace, too, the course of each writer's own views about his work and his world.

In addition to combining a uniquely convenient source of such elusive *documentation*, the 'Writer-Files' series also assembles the *information* necessary for readers to pursue further their interest in a particular writer or work. Variations in quantity between one writer's output and another's, differences in temperament which make some readier than others to talk about their work, and the variety of critical response, all mean that the presentation and balance of material shifts between one volume and another: but we have tried to arrive at a format for the series which will nevertheless enable users of one volume readily to find their way around any other.

Section 1, 'A Brief Chronology', provides a quick conspective overview of each playwright's life and career. *Section 2* deals with the plays themselves, arranged chronologically in the order of their composition: information on first performances, major revivals, and publication is followed by a brief synopsis (for quick reference set in slightly larger, italic type), then by a representative selection of the critical response, and of the dramatist's own comments on the play and its theme.

Section 3 offers concise guidance to each writer's work in non-dramatic forms, while *Section 4*, 'The Writer on His Work', brings together comments from the playwright himself on more general matters of construction, opinion, and artistic development. Finally, *Section 5* provides a bibliographical guide to other primary and secondary sources of further reading, among which full details will be found of works cited elsewhere under short titles, and of collected editions of the plays — but not of individual titles, particulars of which will be found with the other factual data in Section 2.

The 'Writer-Files' hope by striking this kind of balance between information and a wide range of opinion to offer 'companions' to the study of major playwrights in the modern repertoire — not in that dangerous pre-digested fashion which

General Editor's Introduction

5

can too readily quench the desire to read the plays themselves, nor so prescriptively as to allow any single line of approach to predominate, but rather to encourage readers to form their own judgements of the plays in a wide-ranging context.

Peter Nichols has suffered the fate of many innovative artists, as aspects of his work once felt to be liberating become through familiarity to seem primitive intimations of themselves. His recognition of the moment of personal growth that occurred when he stopped trying to write natural-istic plays for television and began 'wondering what was left for theatre to do' coincided with his need to come to terms with the birth of a handicapped child: and the result, in *A Day in the Death of Joe Egg*, was direct engagement with an audience half-embarrassed and half-charmed into complicity. What was new was not the method in itself, deeply rooted as it was in 'the kind of theatre I enjoyed before seeing plays – variety, revue, magic shows, and pantomimes', but its application to a subject seemingly tailor-made for the naturalistic 'problem play' format.

Nichols's serio-comic style, which in *Joe Egg* had deflected the cruelty in the laughter against himself, seemed to me forced and inap-propriate when applied to the wider canvas of *The National Health* – though later, in *Poppy*, he tackled a socio-historical theme more success-fully, and was (in my view) properly offended when its director refused him the tongue-in-cheek tattiness the play required. But in *Privates on Parade* he found a subject which complemented the form so perfectly that we ceased to notice its originality – while more typically, in *Born in the Gardens* and *Passion Play*, audiences have again been startled into fresh insights on familiar situations and emotions.

Nichols's plays have thus tended to remain autobiographical in inspi-ration – which has forced him to confront the familiar problem of the middle-aged professional writer as 'autobiography' narrows itself to the limits expected of a middle-aged professional writer. And it has argu-ably become a danger as well as a strength that his voice is so instantly recognizable to those of his own generation, or with parental or other close associations with its experiences: for, while validating and explor-ing those experiences is an entirely legitimate and desirable function of art, if that art is to endure it has also to be able to connect with new, younger audiences. Irving Wardle thus suggests (on page 43) that Nichols's plays represent, honourably but ephemerally, 'the high-water mark of middle-class society drama' for his own age – while they appear to such as Michael Feingold (on page 55) to deal with 'pain fielded rather than faced'. However, as the record of 'middle-class society drama' from Wycherley to Sheridan to Shaw affirms, theatricality – Nichols's enduring strength – long survives whatever is transitory in social tone.

Simon Trussler

1927   31 July, born in Bristol, son of Richard George Nichols, commercial traveller, and Violet Annie Poole.

1936-44   Pupil at Bristol Grammar School.

1945-48   National Service in Royal Air Force. Serves in India and Malaya. Joins CSE (Combined Services Entertainment) unit and meets Kenneth Williams and Stanley Baxter.

1948-50   Studies at Bristol Old Vic Theatre School. Writing sketches and plays.

1950-55   Various acting jobs from fit-up company in Exeter to work in TV and as film extra.

1955   Goes to Italy to work for Berlitz Language School organization in Milan and Florence.

1955-57   Attends Trent Park Teachers' Training College. Writes short stories.

1957-59   Teaches in primary and secondary modern schools in London.

1959   *Walk on the Grass* televised after winning a BBC West Region competition. *After All* (with Bernie Cooper) televised. Lung collapses. *Promenade* televised. Marries Thelma Reed.

1960   Birth of first child, Abigail.

1961   Receives Arts Council bursary. Abigail suffers fits and brain damage. *Ben Spray*, *The Reception*, and *The Big Boys* televised.

1962   *The Heart of the Country* and *Ben Again* televised.

1963   *Continuity Man* and *The Hooded Terror* televised.

1964   *The Brick Umbrella* televised.

1965   *The Hooded Terror* adapted for stage and performed by Bristol Old Vic Company. *When the Wind Blows* televised. Screenplay for *Catch Us If You Can (Having a Wild Weekend)*.

1966 Screenplay for *Georgy Girl* (with Margaret Forster).

1967 *A Day in the Death of Joe Egg* staged by Glasgow Citizens' Theatre and later transferred to Comedy Theatre, London. Receives John Whiting and *Evening Standard* awards.

1968 *The Gorge* and *Daddy Kiss It Better* televised.

1969 *The National Health* staged by National Theatre. Receives *Evening Standard* award.

1970 *Hearts and Flowers* televised.

1970-76 Member, Board of Governors, Greenwich Theatre.

1971 Directs *A Day in the Death of Joe Egg* for Greenwich. *Forget-Me-Not Lane* staged at Greenwich. Death of daughter, Abigail.

1972 *A Day in the Death of Joe Egg* released by Columbia Pictures. *Neither Up Nor Down* staged at Almost Free Theatre, Soho.

1972-75 Member, Arts Council Drama Panel.

1973 *The National Health* released by Columbia Pictures.

1974 *Chez Nous* staged at Globe Theatre. *The Freeway* staged at National Theatre. *Harding's Luck* staged at Greenwich.

1975 *The Common* televised.

1977 *Privates on Parade* staged by Royal Shakespeare Company at Aldwych Theatre. Receives Society of West End Theatre, *Evening Standard*, and Ivor Novello awards. Visiting Playwright, Guthrie Theatre, Minneapolis, USA, and co-directs *The National Health* in Minneapolis.

1979 Directs *Born in the Gardens* at Bristol Old Vic.

1980 *Born in the Gardens* transferred to Globe Theatre.

1981 *Passion Play* staged by RSC at Aldwych.

1982 *Poppy* staged by RSC at Barbican. *Evening Standard* and Society of West End Theatre awards.

1983   *Privates on Parade* released by Handmade Films. Becomes Fellow of the Royal Society of Literature.

1984   Screenplay for *Changing Places*. Autobiography, *Feeling You're Behind*, published.

1985   Collection of short stories, *Tales From the Waterfront*, published.

1987   *A Piece of My Mind* staged at Apollo Theatre. *Plays: One* published (US edition, 1986).

1990   Directs revival of *Forget-Me-Not Lane* at Greenwich Theatre.

1991   *Plays: Two* published, with new edition of *Plays: One*, revised and introduced by Nichols.

a: Television Plays and Screenplays

After All

A play for television, written in collaboration with Bernie Cooper.
Transmitted: BBC West, Bristol, 1959.
Unpublished.

Promenade

A play for television.
Transmitted: Granada TV, 22 May 1959 (dir. Julian Aymes; with Susannah York as Tricia Blake, William Young as Nicky Blake, Tom Bell as Andrew Turtle, Trader Faulkner as Maurice Goodman, Pauline Yates as Rhonda Holloway, Peter McEnery as Cy Whelan, and Sydonie Platt as Lotte).
Published: Six Granada Plays, Faber, 1960.

A group of young people in their early twenties spend a weekend at a south coast seaside town. The theme of breaking from 'the crowd' for courtship and marriage involves the affection of a major's daughter, Tricia, for Andrew, a manual labourer, and the incapacity for love of Tricia's brother, Nicky, despite his relationship with Rhonda. The latter theme becomes an abiding concern in Nichols's plays.

Penetrating and well written. . . . Julian Aymes's production set far too rapid a pace to begin with and was dogged throughout by faulty balance between cast and music. Visually it was admirably stylish, and caught moments of desperate boredom and forced gaiety with unerring precision.

The Times, 23 May 1959

It described a weekend spent in Brighton with Bernie [Cooper] and Gordon [friends]. The cast were all in their teens and twenties and I wondered if the infant Susannah York was old enough to consider marriage, then found she had a husband already. I'd had to alter the most colourful character from Jew to Gentile so as not to offend . . . the managing director.

Nichols, *Feeling You're Behind*, p. 196, 198

My own . . . preference for television plays is for that kind of mood play in which the plot may be indiscernible and structure invisible. *Promenade* . . . is very much a play of this kind. . . . It has also . . . the special merit of neither belonging to, nor imitating any particular school of television playwriting. It is constructed with deceptive casualness. . . . Its theme . . . lingers . . . so that at the end of the play one's impressions become stronger and continue to expand in the imagination, enriching the meaning of what has gone before.

Julian Aymes,
Six Granada Plays, p. 45

When I saw *Promenade* . . . my immediate reaction was a desire to work with this writer myself. Here was someone who really understood how to use the medium of television and who wrote in a style that was both authentic and contemporary.

Cliff Owen,
New Granada Plays, p. 187

Walk on the Grass

A play for television.
Transmitted: BBC West, Bristol, 1959.
Unpublished.

The play is an impression of family life, the families being those of Peter Nichols and his brother, Geoffrey. The play won the BBC West Region contest and seems to be influenced by Chekhov, Turgenev, Ibsen, and Paddy Chayevsky.

11

It makes dull reading now but was a step in the right direction —
towards reality.

Nichols, *Feeling You're Behind*, p. 196

Ben Spray

A play for television.

Transmitted: Granada TV, 23 Feb. 1961 (dir. Cliff Owen; with Derrick
   Sherwin as Dave Riley, Ian Hendry as Ben Spray, Jane Jordan Rogers
   as Louise Stone, Lockwood West as John Stone, Betty Huntley-
   Wright as Hazel Stone, John Arnatt as Daniel Hamilton, Philip Bond
   as Geof, Jennifer Schooling as Veronica, Mavis Ranson as Tibby,
   Joanna Vogel as Patricia, John Gayford as First Man, Elizabeth Wills
   as First Woman, Anthony Dawes as Second Man, Annika Wills as
   Second Woman, and Felicity Young as Waitress).
Revived: ATV, 1971.
Published: New Granada Plays, Faber, 1961.

*Ben Spray, 'romantic, nervous, desperate', shares a flat in
Fulham with coarsely handsome Dave Riley, 'realistic, selfish,
assured'. On Guy Fawkes night Ben prepares for a date with the
attractive Pat while she prepares to meet a rich man, sending
her flatmate, the plain Louise, to deliver a note to Ben. Ben,
after venting his anger and insecurities, goes with Louise to her
uncle John Stone's fireworks party. In this suburban setting, Ben
meets other family members, dances with the attractive Veronica
(Ronnie), and accidentally sends a plate of food flying, when
Louise enters from the kitchen. Geof, a callow Cambridge
undergraduate, argues with Ben about immigrants during an
attempt at a game of charades. Later, in the garden, Louise tells
Ben he is immature; he goes in search of the bathroom before
leaving, but encounters eight-year-old Tibby, talks to her, and
innocently lies on her bed, whereupon Hazel looks in and
assumes the worst. Ben escapes from the ensuing chaos. Next
day, in contrast to a hungover Dave, Ben is sprightly and
excited at the prospect of a new job as cinema commissionaire.*

We hated each other at first sight . . . but I soon saw what he had to teach me: wit and style. Bernie Cooper was cool. . . . He put me in touch with jazz again — but Dave Brubeck and the MJQ. . . . Bernie is a natural educator. His latest letter to me came yesterday from Bangkok, where he is living with and helping a community of slum-dwellers, expressing his state of mind at reaching fifty: 'still cool, still ambivalent', or — as I described him as the hero of my play *Ben Spray* — the oldest teenager in the business.

Nichols, *Feeling You're Behind*, p. 170-1

When *Ben Spray* arrived my first feeling was one of extreme apprehension.

The script had all the verbal brilliance one could expect — a splendidly comedic expression of the frustrations and calculated nonconformism of young people today. But Ben Spray is not just another ageing youth with a chip on his shoulder. He is an intelligent 26-year-old desperately trying to find within himself a personality he can accept as an adult.

The problem was where would we find an actor who could explore the rich possibilities such a part offered. Ben Spray was a person and the actor had to be at least as real as the script. Then Ian Hendry read the part and the search was over.

His brilliant, very human, and finely detailed performance ensured the play's success and will stay long in my mind.

Cliff Owen, *New Granada Plays*, p. 187

Ben Spray . . . is an innocent but an indestructible innocent. . . . This was Mr. Nichols's most accomplished television play yet (he seems happiest in comedy). . . . Pace was essential to the play's effect, and Mr. Cliff Owen's direction never once allowed it to flag.

The Times, 24 Feb. 1961

A Diabolical Liberty

A play for television.
Transmitted: Granada, 5 May 1961.
Unpublished.

Independent television brought us Mr. Peter Nichols in

experimental mood with his dramatic 'comic strip', A Diabolical Liberty.

The Times, 19 May 1961

[The above statement, suggesting that the play was transmitted on or around 5 May 1961, was dropped from the 20 May 1961 edition of *The Times,* which carried virtually the same review of *The Reception* from which this reference was taken. In the absence of an explanation by Peter Nichols, one can only conclude that the attribution in *The Times* of such a play to him is an error or that he did write the play but something prevented its performance at the last minute. It does not appear in the listings of television programmes around the date in question.]

The Reception

A play for television.
Transmitted: Granada, 18 May 1961.
Unpublished.

An essay in . . . broad farce about a wedding that goes wrong. Things start going awry when the bride's former fiancé turns up uninvited with a present: a portrait of the bride in her underwear (so much more suggestive than a nude).

The Times, 19 May 1961

'He's being victimized', shrills the groom's mother (Miss Olga Lindo) a frosty, befeathered matron in the best farcical tradition. Confusion reigns; rival factions locked in bedroom and bathroom turn on bride and groom.

Unfortunately at this point Mr. Nichols lets his situation get out of hand, and not even the first excruciating moments of a party game involving a trio of fractious aunts can save it.

The Times, 20 May 1961

A broad farce about a wedding that goes wrong prepares for Nichols's later flights of fancy in which everyday life is overwhelmed by the bizarre. It also paves the way for the atmosphere of not-so-quiet dismay in which the grotesque appears in a way that seems almost natural.

Enoch Brater, 'Peter Nichols',
*Dictionary of Literary Biography, Vol. XIII, Part 2:
British Dramatists since World War II*, p. 355

The Big Boys

A play for television.
Transmitted: BBC, 28 Aug. 1961 (with Roy Holder as Alan Ruddle and Leslie Sands as Douglas Driver).
Unpublished.

The play draws on Nichols's experience as a school teacher to give a picture of an adulterous teacher and a suicidal schoolboy.

Dramatizes a mutually destructive relationship between a child and an adult.

Enoch Brater, 'Peter Nichols', p. 355

One of the small boys in a London school . . . took a mild poison because he was afraid of forgetting his lines in the school pantomime. The state of mind or attitude determining this action was never brought home to us. The author's failure to suggest how the mind of one of his big boys — that is, masters at the school — worked on discovering his wife's love affair with a colleague was more damaging still.

The Times, 29 Aug. 1961

The world of school is full of dramatic possibilities and advantages . . . an invention as happy and fertile as the discovery of the court-room scene.
   However, the world being unluckily what it is . . . new theme becomes . . . old theme and needs . . . real originality of treatment to redeem it theatrically. . . . *The Big Boys* . . . to a certain extent brought

this off. . . . Freshness of approach went some way towards saving the day. The *cocu* was individually drawn and excellently played by Leslie Sands. There was a telling scene in which a wretched little boy (another assured performance by Roy Holder), suffering from stage-fright at the Christmas pantomime, creeps into the changing room to eat mistletoe berries. And there was a proper avoidance of the . . . sugary ending. . . . Not great drama.

Hilary Cork,
The Listener, 7 Sept. 1961

Ben Again

A play for television.
Transmitted: Granada TV, 1962.
Unpublished.

The Heart of the Country

A play for television.
Transmitted: ATV, 1962.
Unpublished.

Written with the working title The Mouse Race, *the play is about small town life in the south west, and one character is based on a neighbour of Nichols at the time, Christopher Milne.*

One of the characters is based on Christopher Robin Milne . . . or rather . . . on the idea of being a public child.

Nichols, *Feeling You're Behind*, p. 208

Of all his works, as its resonant title suggests, it was '. . . the most ambitious so far . . .' but was '. . . ruined by its performance'.

Nichols, *Feeling You're Behind*, p. 208

Continuity Man

A play for television, originally written for the stage.
Transmitted: BBC TV, 10 Mar. 1963 (dir. Christopher Morahan;
    with Roger Livesey as the Father, Richard Pasco as Don,
    Susan Maryott as Rosamund, and Moira Redmond as the
    Film Star).
Unpublished.

*This is Nichols's first completed play to dramatize his father's
personality. The role was played by Roger Livesey.*

In London I heard that no one liked *Continuity Man*. . . . Too mild,
everyone said. Peggy Ramsay [Nichols's agent] told me: 'Your trouble,
Peter, is you're not wicked enough. There's not enough vice in you.'
That there's truth in her comments is all the more upsetting — but how
do you start being wicked all of a sudden? Buy the Illustrated Home
Abortionist? Or is Abo [Abigail, his severely handicapped daughter] a
more pathetic victim? Perhaps go after other women or get drunk?
I drink and flirt averagely. I was averagely ungrateful to my parents. I'm
not generous and was till a year ago selfish and ambitious. When I lost
my ambition I began to grow up. Probably it was only Peggy's way of
saying the play stank. . . .

> Nichols, *Feeling You're Behind*, p. 210-11

Don . . . a radio 'disc jockey' and 'continuity man', and Rosamund . . .
his wife, are running at high speed from their lower middle-class
origins. . . . Their unsatisfactory equilibrium is disturbed first by Don's
father . . . a crotchety, talkative, upright vulgarian, and then by a
beautiful film star . . . whom Don has to interview.

Mr. Nichols lays down the situation firmly and sensitively, but when
he brings his quartet together . . . [the] big scene refuses to grow to the
required size. More wit in the talk and more freedom of visual comment
from Mr. Christopher Morahan's production might have persuaded us
that Don had sufficient cause to come to his senses. The actors worked
well but with too little material.

> *The Times,* 12 Mar. 1963

17

The Hooded Terror

A play for television.

Transmitted: ATV, 25 Aug. 1963 (dir. Christopher Morahan; with John
   Ronane as the Boxer and Michael Wynne, Patricia Haines, John
   Wood, and Jennie Linden as the two couples).
Stage version: Bristol Old Vic, 1964.
Unpublished.

---

*Two young couples, one week-ending with the other, meet a
hooded boxer in a local funfair and bring him back with them
to give their babysitter a fright. But our expectations of this
situation are neatly reversed: the apparently normal, agreeable
couples prove to be torn apart by jealousy and prejudice, all of
which is unleashed by the new situation the appearance of the
boxer in their midst creates, while the boxer himself, for all his
sinister aspect, turns out to be a true innocent, an honest and
idealistic young man who feels an immense nostalgia for the
settled family life he imagines he will find in his hosts' house.*

John Russell Taylor, *The Second Wave*
(Methuen, 1971), p. 19

This TV thriller is set in Dartmouth. Nichols adapted it for the stage,
commenting that 'I wrongly felt the plot was strong enough to bear
stretching to a full-length stage play, which was put on in a token season
of local plays at the Old Vic's second house.

Nichols, *Feeling You're Behind*, p. 215

The small screen is . . . adept at probing beneath the urbane surface of
ordinary everyday behaviour, which is Mr. Nichols's purpose here.
   Mr. Nichols attempts to make this revelation gripping by pointing to
the potential destructiveness lying in the unconscious of ordinary folk.

The Times, 26 Aug. 1963

The Brick Umbrella

A play for television
Transmitted: ATV, 31 May 1964 (dir. Christopher Morahan).

When Peter [Nichols] and I worked together at ATV on plays like *The Brick Umbrella* and *The Hooded Terror*, producers didn't seem to be very thick on the ground. We were very used to taking our own decisions and also being critical with each other. Tony [Garnett] in those circumstances was a marvellous producer. He creates the circumstances in which people can make films successfully, and acts all the time as an objective judge and adviser.

Christopher Morahan, interviewed by Paul Madden, July 1976,
'Complete Programme Notes for a Season of British Television Drama
1959-1973', National Film Theatre, 11-24 Oct. 1976,
in National Film Archive

We know Mr. Nichols, of course, as a cunning dramatic manipulator of social embarrassments, usually with the hero playing a large part in setting them up. On this occasion, though, the hero is on the receiving end: he is the embarrassed odd man out at a wedding party where he is giving away the bride — his wife's friend, whom he has not met before.

It might have made a jolly hour's television, but somehow it did not. . . . Christopher Morahan's direction went in, gamely but without flair, for showy cut-in 'thinks' shots to make it all look bright and contemporary. The cast battled valiantly but in vain.

The Times, 1 June 1964

[The slightly longer review that appeared the following day added more detail.]

[The hero] gets slightly involved with the bride before the ceremony, and gets on the wrong side of groom and groom's friends (a group, admittedly, of dreary hearties who would hardly bring out the social side of any moderately sane person). . . . He also fails to extract a loan from the bride's father, which was the main purpose of his visit. . . .

Mr. Nichols seemed quite incapable of making up his mind about the class, background, or even period of his characters. . . . Every occasion

19

for liberal fidgets — anti-semitism, homosexuality, public schools, social sadism of all sorts — was dragged in. . . .

The Times, 2 June 1964

When the Wind Blows

A play for television.
Transmitted: ATV, 2 Aug. 1965 (dir. Graham Evans; with Alec
    McCowen as Ralph Quantick, or 'Q', Eileen Atkins as Norma,
    Q's wife, Alison Leggatt as Evelyn, his mother, and Ralph
    Michael as Albert, his father).
Radio version: BBC West.
Unpublished.

*A domestic quartet describing a visit Thelma [Nichols's wife]
and I might have made to Palatine Lodge [his parents' home in
Bristol], very well played. . . .*

Nichols, *Feeling You're Behind*, p. 216

I didn't have much to do with the production. . . . Graham Evans came down to visit me in Bristol. . . . We talked about the play, and he went away and did it . . . he did it so well. The rooms in *When the Wind Blows* do look cramped, because Graham Evans stood the cameras back.

I think the impression of the mother's room is very good — it's just what those rooms look like. Theatre critics always remark on the formality of my stage plays and I've agreed and pointed out that my television plays are very straight, and naturalistic. I realize, seeing *When the Wind Blows*, that that's not so. It's got the device of the child, not shown in vision, voice-over, talking to the audience, soliloquy. A shorthand's developed both for film and the stage, and I'd now leave much more to the audience to get. The play is a bit theatrical, which is why it transferred well to the stage in *Forget-Me-Not Lane* — that has many more devices, but the essence of both is the same. I wrote *When the Wind Blows* in a fortnight, which was unusually fast for me, and I'd thought of it in the form it eventually appeared.

Nichols, interviewed by Paul Madden, May 1976,
'Complete Programme Notes for a Season of British Television
Drama 1959-1973', National Film Theatre, 11-24 Oct. 1976,
in National Film Archive

The drama presents two couples, one young, one middle-aged, and builds suspense by delaying its dénouement until the very end, where a surprise finale brings destruction to the marriage of the older couple, where it was least suspected. Nichols's plays for television therefore predict those situations, characters, obsessions, and motivations associated with his far more famous work for the West End.

Enoch Brater,'Peter Nichols', p. 356

Mr. Nichols's onslaught on domesticity is energetic and witty, happily unafraid of intellectual conversation. . . . Graham Evans's direction gained a few slick laughs from its baby's-eye-view of irritated parents and doting grandparents, but was relevantly witty in the treatment of maddening simultaneous conversations.

The Times, 3 Aug. 1965

Catch Us If You Can
(Having a Wild Weekend)

Film script.
Released: Burton Film Productions, April 1965; distributed in the USA by Warner Brothers, 1965, as *Having a Wild Weekend* (dir. John Boorman; with Dave Clark and the Dave Clark Five; Dave Clark as Steve, Yootha Joyce as Nan, Robert Lang as Whiting, and Clive Swift as Duffle).
Unpublished.

We wrote the script from scratch in a month, a pretentious odyssey about middle-aged entrepreneurs exploiting young talent, crammed with irony, philosophic overtones, and three-syllable words. . . . Only a few lines of mine survived to the finished film, which had a mixed reception, much admired by Brian Forbes. . . .

Nichols, *Feeling You're Behind*, p. 16

We would not, on previous experience, recognize in the bored upper-middle-class husband and wife who pick up the young hero and heroine on their way west and try, not very successfully, to use them as sexual playthings what one might call typical Nichols characters, and yet they are very vividly created — more so, certainly, than the rather colourless juveniles of the piece.

John Russell Taylor, *The Second Wave*
(Methuen, 1971), p. 22

The Gorge

A play for television.
Transmitted: BBC TV, 4 Sept. 1968 (dir. Christopher Morahan; with Billy Harmon as Mike, Constance Chapman as Lily, Reg Lye as Jack, Neil Wilson as Stanley, Betty Alberge as Ivy, Elna Pearl as Chris, John Woodnutt as Norman, Hilda Braid as Joyce, David Webb as Cyclist, and Brian Gear as Potholer).
Published: Robert Muller, ed., *The Television Dramatist*, 1973.

A filmed account of a family picnic, where the action of the outing to Cheddar Gorge and the subsequent picnic is interspersed with clips from the father, Stanley's, home movie. Through Mike, Nichols explores the tension between the know-it-all father and his morose son, whose own agenda is not so much the picnic but a secret meeting with a pretty girl, Chris, his junior in years, but emotionally and sexually his senior.

I had a lot to do with the making of the play. Chris Morahan and I chose all the locations together, and I was there all the time. A lot had to be left to Chris as director. I'd described the mechanics of the picnic, and of the farce, but he had to invent a heck of a lot.

The home-movies idea was based on my parents-in-law. . . . The lovely thing is they're always arguing about where it is, they never know where it was taken — the whole of Europe is a kind of backdrop for their home-movies. It's nice when you can interest the audience in the technique of using things like home-movies.

I think the method pays off very well at the end of the play. We've seen all the embarrassment about the trousers, the bossy father hasn't.

Then they have the crash, and he goes round the car, and pulls open the door and the girl's father is sitting there without his trousers because he's given his trousers to his daughter who has lost her skirt [jeans in the text]. That paid off very well, but the crash was an addition I put in later on. We had to stage the traffic jam, and they had an AA man to direct the traffic. While he was doing it he was going around to all the cars of the technicians trying to sell them AA membership! That's included at the end as an actual bit of business.

Nichols, interviewed by Paul Madden, May 1976,
'Complete Programme Notes for a Season of British Television
Drama 1959-1973', National Film Theatre, 11-24 Oct. 1976,
in National Film Archive

The germ of this play/film/story was pitching the tent and cooking and eating the Sunday roast. What came before and after that was, as usual with me, a jigsaw of dimly remembered episodes, landscapes, and people. I did tear my trousers in a public place and was too embarrassed to walk through the crowd; I chased a girl among the ferns of the Mendips; on the Bristol Downs, our Speakers' Corner during the war, we tormented the evangelists; one of my pets was a grass snake. Childhood excursions in the Morris Twelve were often to Cheddar Gorge, where we oohed and aahed at the Underwater Cathedral or the Alpine Village; where the restaurant's roof was a goldfish tank and its liquid light fell on a white piano.

Nichols, *The Television Dramatist*, p. 73

[Nichols] was concerned with the damage done to sensitive, intelligent adolescents by their dull, grey parents, and succeeded, with skill and a good deal of daring, for his views of family life are not exactly orthodox, in looking at the adult world through the eyes of an intelligent boy of sixteen.

Mr. Nichols knows that adolescents suffer from high standards, and understands exactly why Mike is outraged by his family's way of life, by the show, the pointless complications which make a picnic unenjoyable, the mindless vulgarity which his own party shares with other picnickers; Mr. Nichols sympathizes with the boy, and persuades us to do the same.

Henry Raynor,
The Times, 5 Sept. 1968.

23

Georgy Girl

Film script, in collaboration with Margaret Forster, based on her novel
    of the same name (Secker and Warburg).
Released: Columbia, May 1966 (dir. Silvio Narizzano; with Lynn
    Redgrave as Georgy, James Mason as James Leamington, Alan Bates
    as Jos, Charlotte Rampling as Meredith, Rachel Kempson as Ellen,
    and Dandy Nichols as Nurse).
Musical: as *Georgy*, Winter Garden, New York, 26 Feb. 1970 (based on
    the film; with book by Tom Mankiewicz and Carole Bayer; music by
    George Fischoff). Nichols was not involved in this work.

Daddy Kiss It Better

A play for television.
Transmitted: Yorkshire Television, 29 July 1968 (dir. Christopher
    Hodson; with Michael Craig as Ken and Dilys Laye as Monica).
Unpublished.

---

*The plot . . . presents the breakup of a marriage in a
kaleidoscopic pattern of flashbacks, where once again the
dominant theme is the mutually destructive relations of parents
and children.*

Enoch Brater, 'Peter Nichols', p. 59

[The play is an impression of the life of] a Nichols hero — 35, married,
one or two kids, own car, own mortgage, £1,200 a year, and the sardonic
melancholy of a man who can see himself in sharp outline. . . .

In *A Day in the Death of Joe Egg* the hero was stretched on the rack
of a strong dramatic situation. Here, as in the memorable *When the
Wind Blows* of a couple of years ago, he just soldiers on, ruefully
wondering why he volunteered. Nothing very much 'happens' in either
of these two excellent plays, but I can't think of many things more
dramatic than the thought of ten million people sitting safe around their
TV sets and discovering that someone has got them right between the
eyes.

Tom Stoppard, *The Observer*, 4 August, 1968

Mr. Nichols's play is a kaleidoscope of. . . [Ken's] memories, in which marriage is only the most painful of his many failures. Mr. Nichols presents all the elements of the case quietly, kindly, and with unobtrusive humour; he finds a hopeful solution emerging from matrimonial brinkmanship.

Henry Raynor,
The Times, 30 July 1968

Majesty

Adaptation for television, from the story by Scott Fitzgerald.
Transmitted: BBC 2, 17 Oct. 1968

Majesty *tells the story of a rich girl's revolt against a New York dynastic marriage. She flees to Europe, lives it up in Paris, but redeems herself by making a Grace Kelly marriage to a comic opera prince. The romantic inflation which in* Gatsby *gives mystery and resonance to the story, becomes an aid to snobbery in* Majesty. . . . *Peter Nichols's dramatizing of* Majesty *was very well done and Shirley Knight had just the right hysterical edge for Emily.*

Peter Porter, *New Statesman*, 18 Oct. 1968

Winner Takes All

A play for television, from a story by Evelyn Waugh.
Transmitted: 1968.

Hearts and Flowers

A play for television.
Transmitted: BBC TV, 3 Dec. 1970, repeat broadcast 1971 (dir.
  Christopher Morahan; with Anthony Hopkins as Bob, Priscilla
  Morgan as Jean, Constance Chapman as Marie, Donald Churchill as
  Tony, Leon Cortez as Will, Eric Francis as Lionel, Clifford Parish as
  Eric, Betty Bascombe as Phyllis, Freda Bamford as Vera, Sheila

Keith as Una, Martin Wyldeck as Mr. Fowler, Grace Arnold as Mrs. Fowler, Jeffrey Segal as Witts, Maryann Turner as Linda, Bill Horsley as Vicar, April Wilding as Woman at Station, and Roy Hepworth as Mr. Brittain).
Published: Robert Wade, ed., *The Television Play* (BBC, 1976); *Plays: One.*

Bob lives in Bristol and teaches in a secondary school. His elder brother Tony left home years ago and is a well-known television journalist and presenter. Bob suspects and derides Tony's facile sentiments. . . . But he's envious at the same time — of Tony's success. . . . As the play goes on, we learn of his deeper reasons for resenting his brother — that Bob's wife Jean married him after being jilted by Tony and harbours an unsatisfied longing for the elder man.

Tony and Bob are two aspects of myself. Like everyone I know — including my brother — I am a divided character, hoping for an exciting and passionate life but equally enjoying the claims of work and duty. The play is based on that tension and the father's funeral is the setting which brings it briefly to the surface.

Nichols, *Plays: One* (1987), p. 87-8

The production was brilliant and had a fine cast, headed by Anthony Hopkins as Bob, a natural Mark Antony playing Cassius, bringing the part a sort of prosaic passion. Even so, as usual, the Bristolian background . . . was more or less ignored. The funeral was shot, not among the bizarre monuments of Arno's Vale but at Norwood. Among the cast, only Constance Chapman as Marie was able to speak with the right accent. What would they say of a Scouse [Liverpool] play where everyone spoke Welsh or Posh?

Nichols, *Plays: One* (1987), p. 88

More telephone calls came than for any previous TV play I'd had on. Harold Pinter rang to say it hit him North, South, East, and West.

Nichols, *Plays: One* (1987), p. 88

The British Film Institute applied to the BBC to include this production in a season of television plays for the National Film Theatre. They were told that it had been wiped. . . . A week or two after writing this, I was sent a black and white copy, taken from the first transmission.

Nichols, *Plays: One* (1987), p. 89

Nichols takes us, factually and chronologically, through the events surrounding death . . . all the hypocrisy of ill-assorted relatives, mouthing platitudes and trying the dead man's tennis shoes for size, and all the superficially cathartic effects of a family death on the remaining members of the group.

Nichols's brilliance is such that he manages to convey all this without ever putting a single phrase into a single mouth which is out of tune with his characters — his ear for the clichés and truisms of every-day speech is superb.

Chris Dunkley, *The Times*, 4 Dec. 1970

The Common

A play for television.
Transmitted: BBC TV, 20 Oct. 1973 (dir. Christopher Morahan;
    with Vivien Merchant, Peter Jeffrey, Denis Waterman, and Gwen
    Taylor).
Published: Plays: One (1987). This is the original version submitted to
    the BBC but rejected in favour of a rewritten, different play which
    Nichols describes below as *The Common 2.*

In The Common *the butt is a . . . general social hypocrisy. Jane and Edward Noble live in style on the edge of the (Blackheath, Hampstead name your own) common while setting up a hostel for ex-prisoners in someone else's street (so sad, but property prices you know). Meanwhile young schoolteacher Sean Lamb 'improvises' revolutionary school plays with his kids, provoking them to break into Edward's place — the night he's away and Jane's entertaining Sean. And the spell-casting black man who has actually exercised his right to squat on the ancient common they are all so worked up about as a symbol of sharing and freedom gets towed away by the police.*

An exercise in uncertainties then — of working-class Tories and property-hooked Liberals, susceptible socialists, anti-social environmentalists, even a liberated kept woman. And the whole thing drives forward on Nichols's very personal mixture of dramatic skills — comedy and caricature interwoven with declamation, observation and straight old-fashioned crowd-pulling sex.

Peter Fiddick,
The Guardian, 22 Oct. 1973

He [Peter Nichols] went at the diagnosis [of our social distempers] bald-headed. His rich young couple from the big house up by the common came down to indulge their social conscience where it would not affect their comfort. Their proposal for a hostel for ex–offenders brought a public meeting at the Wat Tyler School. And there they met the Socialist teacher who was living in sin and a basement flat.

After that . . . we had argument on everything from the laws of property to race relations. . . . . Chiefly . . . we were concerned with the gulf in our society and the compromises that rich and poor make to live.

Vivien Merchant and Peter Jeffrey as the rich pair with Dennis Waterman as the teacher and Gwen Taylor as his girl friend were all excellent, and the author's comic invention never flagged. But the characters were really caricatures of social attitudes and the whole thing wore an air of parody that started by being funnny, became quaint, and ended by being absurd.

Besides, the debate played the devil with the drama. Passion halted at the bedpost while the parties discussed Karl Marx. . . . 'I'm treating you like a polytechnic', the teacher said . . . to the voluptuous Miss Merchant. The suspicion grew that Mr. Nichols was doing that to the rest of us too.

Leonard Buckley,
The Times, 22 Oct. 1973

The BBC had got two plays for the price of one and, of course, the one they produced was much more to their taste. It was ironic, paradoxical, took no sides and was about as far from my original intention as *The Sound of Music*. A comparison of the two plays is an instructive reminder of how gentle the Thought Police can be. *The Common 2* may be a better play, so much so that Rattigan urged me to adapt it for the stage. *The Common 1* is a better film and sticks to its guns and, as it's never been seen, I am glad of the chance to have it published.

Nichols, *Plays: One* (1987), p. 243

Changing Places

Film: screenplay, from the novel by David Lodge.
Released: 1984.

b: Stage Plays

A Day in the Death of Joe Egg

A play in two acts.
First production: Citizens' Th., Glasgow, 9 May 1967 (dir. Michael
    Blakemore; with Joe Melia as Bri, Zena Walker as Sheila, Barbara
    Goldman as Joe, Carole Boyer as Pam, Michael Murray as Freddie,
    and Joan Hickson as Grace), trans. Comedy Th., London, 20 July
    1967 (with Phyllida Law as Pam, Elaine Mileham or Susan Porter
    as Joe, and John Carson as Freddie).
Revivals: Greenwich Th., 1971 (dir. Peter Nichols; with Caroline
    Mortimer as Sheila and Ray Brooks as Bri). Many other productions
    throughout the world: the play has been translated widely, and is a
    regular source of income.
First New York production: Brooks Atkinson Th., 1 Feb. 1968 (dir.
    Michael Blakemore; with Albert Finney as Bri and Susan Alpern
    as Joe).
Revivals: Roundabout Th., 1985, trans. Longacre Th., 27 Mar. 1985
    (dir. Arvin Brown; with Jim Dale as Bri and Stockard Channing as
    Sheila).
Film: Domino-Columbia Pictures 1971 (script by Nichols;
    dir. Peter Medak; with Alan Bates as Bri, Janet Suzman as Sheila,
    and Joan Hickson as Grace).
Published: Faber, 1967; *Plays: One* (1991).

*Bri, a teacher in a secondary modern school, and his pretty wife
Sheila have a mentally handicapped child. The play shows them
coping with this heartrending situation by means of jokes and
satirical conversation pieces directed at the inadequacies of
clergy, doctors, nurses, and hospitals, while their marriage*

breaks up, despite the bond created between them by the brain damaged daughter, 'Joe Egg'.

Talking it over with Bob Bolt later, I said: 'As far as playwriting goes, this kind of accident's useless. There's nothing to be done with it.'. . .

Our aesthetic principle had been to present the facts, get the jokes right, and leave feeling to the audience. . . .

For some time there was the same awkward silence that we'd sometimes met from visitors when we had done our 'act' for them. . . . Then someone broke the ice and soon the laughter came free and full. . . . A microscopic moment of history had passed, a taboo had been broken.

Nichols, *Feeling You're Behind*, p. 213, 225, 227

In the course of wondering what was left for theatre to do, I defined a rough approach to playwriting. I would try to find a role for the spectators. Straightforward in its early drafts, my first real stage play *A Day in the Death of Joe Egg* broke the mirror more and more as I revised it. The audience was shouted at, appealed to, confided in . . . . Either the actors or the characters or the author — probably all — were betraying the implicit licence the audience had granted them: to play the game of illusion by understood rules. But many works of fiction are also critical demonstrations. . . . The problem is not only how to live with a handicapped child but how to describe that life (as the husband puts it) 'in a way that will prevent a stampede to the exit-doors'. Its final draft became a criticism of its first. It's a play about a play.

Nichols, 'Introduction', *Plays: One* (1991), p. xiii

This is one of the rare occasions on which audiences can feel the earth moving under their feet. It marks the theatrical arrival of a young dramatist capable of the hardest task of his trade: treating an intensely painful taboo subject with absolute truthfulness and yet without alienating the public. In achieving this, I believe that Peter Nichols and a dazzling cast have significantly shifted our boundaries of taste.

Peter Nichols has re-established the old truth (which needs constantly to be rediscovered) that comedy has its roots in suffering. . . . [He] has observed the speech habits, social attitudes, and ideological confusions of the British 'sixties, and in his stage presents our own image. This is not avant-garde writing: it is addressed to the general civic conscience, and it endows the random audience with the sense of a common human bond.

Irving Wardle, *The Times*, 21 July, 1967

This remarkable play is about a nightmare all women must have dreamed at some time, and most men; living with a child born so hopelessly crippled as to be, as the father in it says brutally, 'a human parsnip'. For all that it has to be described as a comedy, one of the funniest and most touching I've seen.

Ronald Bryden,
The Observer, 23 July 1967

On the Greenwich revival, directed by Nichols

The spectacle of the child's fits was appalling but not aesthetically disgusting; the play moved me but did not mock my inability to do anything about the situation.

I was able to admire Peter Nichols's sheer skill. . . . In the production at the Comedy the asides did not work happily; on the Greenwich stage actors can naturally address the house.

Nichols the dramatist deserves better of Nichols the director in the second act. Bri's determination first to kill the child then to run away was curiously unpointed last night. It is interesting, and no doubt legitimate, that one is left feeling that Bri will return to his responsibilities; but one should feel that he has wanted to run away.

Charles Lewsen,
The Times, 3 Dec. 1971

On the first New York production

Joe Egg . . . is an immensely moving, even profound play about love and marriage. No, it's not funny — it has wit, a bitter, excoriating wit. No, it's not tragic — it's ironic, as ironic as the uncalled-for domestic accident, the unexpected death in incongruity. . . . What *Joe Egg* attempts, and . . . to a surprising extent achieves, is the analysis of a relationship, the dissection of human feeling, the laying bare of people.

Clive Barnes,
New York Times, 2 Feb. 1968

A Day in the Death of Joe Egg

There is the courage as well as the humour of desperation in *Joe Egg*, and if Bri is defeated, Sheila is not. *Joe Egg* may or may not satisfy you — and disturb you — but there's no doubt about the quality of the performances of Mr. Finney and Miss Walker, or of Mr. Nichols's understanding of human nature.

Richard P. Cooke,
Wall Street Journal, 5 Feb. 1968

There is no head-on solution to the existence of a loved child that will never be anything better than a fair-skinned rag doll. They must turn life itself into theatre in an effort to cope. They must turn into performers for each other. . . . It is a part of the game that must forever go on, life brightly dramatized where it can't be brightly lived.

Under all of this, the ache, of course.

In a particularly brilliant sequence, friend Elizabeth Hubbard cuts short the conventional cooing noises she has been offering the child to insist, at nerve's edge, that she cannot stand anything N.P.A. (Not Personally Attractive, that is). Never could. 'If I say gas chamber, that sounds horrible', she fidgets, pained by her own untidy revulsion, 'but I do mean put them to sleep.' The actress has used the directness of theatre in the heart of a home. The form of Mr. Nichols's play is just. To have made it naturalistic would have been to make it clinical or — worse yet — sentimental. Now it is amiable and angry, standing its ground with a fierce grin.

Walter Kerr,
New York Times, 11 Feb. 1968

On the 1979 production, directed by Sandy Neilson

When Sheila matures enough to accept the facts of her lifelong human burden, Brian, for ever hiding his own fear of inadequacy behind a dementedly comic front, opts out, albeit guiltily, and goes back presumably to his stupid but undemanding mother.

Under Sandy Neilson's direction [at Brunton Theatre] John Bett . . . plays Brian on a razor edge between the fatuous and the genuinely pitiable; and Vari Sylvester, all sharp teeth and bright eyes beneath the tousled hair, suggests a sisterhood with the kitchen cat — both, you feel were born to survive, no matter what.

Cordelia Oliver,
The Guardian, 29 Oct. 1979

The more Mr. Nichols thought about it, the more it seemed to him that naturalism was more of a contrivance, more of a device, than directly addressing the spectators.

'Once I admitted that, the play opened up in all sorts of ways', he remembers. . . . The play gradually became richer, more textured, more ironic, and funnier, much funnier.

Indeed, Mr. Nichols had stumbled on the style that has since served him in stage play after stage play. He reckons that it ultimately derives from one of the key experiences of his youth, seeing Thornton Wilder's *Skin of Our Teeth* with Vivien Leigh as it passed through his native Bristol. 'I thought it marvellous. It was a very serious play, dealing with the history of the human race, but in a comic-strip style. For years it never occurred to me that I could use it. I wasted them writing neat standard plays for TV. But *Joe Egg* forced me to raise myself to a different level. And that's what I've ended up doing, writing comic-strip work in a variety of ways. That, I found, was really my own voice.'

Benedict Nightingale, 'The Birth and Slow Acceptance of *Joe Egg*', *New York Times*, 24 Mar. 1985

The National Health
or Nurse Norton's Affair

A play in two acts.

First production: National Th. at the Old Vic, London, 16 Oct. 1969 (dir. Michael Blakemore; with Jim Dale as Barnet and Cleo Sylvestre as Staff Nurse Norton).

First American production: Long Wharf Th., New Haven, trans. Circle in the Square/Joseph E. Levine Th., New York, 10 Oct. 1974 (dir. Arvin Brown; with Rita Moreno as Staff Nurse Norton and Leonard Frey as Barnet).

Revivals: Guthrie Th., Minneapolis, 1975 (co-dir. Nichols).

Film: Columbia Pictures, Mar. 1973 (screenplay by Nichols; dir. Jack Gold; with Jim Dale as Barnet, and Donald Sinden, Lynn Redgrave, Mervyn Johns, Colin Blakely, and Clive Swift).

Published: Faber, 1970; *Plays: One* (1991).

A comedic dance of death set in a British state hospital. The 'reality' of life in the ward amid the diseased and dying is interspersed with a parody of a television soap opera version of hospital life.

In fact my best play *The End Beds* had been turned down by every script editor in Britain, including those at the BBC, who at once offered to buy the rights when it appeared as *The National Health.*

Nichols, *Feeling You're Behind*, p. 214

The first audience welcomed it like wine. They laughed with recognition from the opening dawn chorus to the chilling finale. Afterwards Olivier hugged me and told me how clever I was. . . .

Nichols, *Plays: One* (1991), p. 116

There are plenty of aesthetic reasons for standing up and cheering this play: but, as in the case of *A Day in the Death of Joe Egg*, it makes you feel ashamed to talk about art. We are not short of good playwrights in Britain, but I know of none with Peter Nichols's power to put modern Britain on the stage and send the spectators away feeling more like members of the human race.

The National Health can only be described as a portrait of six male inmates in a hospital ward. It also amounts to a study of organization versus the individual, and to a microcosm of our society; but such themes only arise from his detailed concern for the people themselves and their response to seeing each other die. . . .

We are with common humanity handled with a touch which Chekhov would have approved.

Irving Wardle,
The Times, 17 Oct. 1969

The National Health at the Old Vic is not a play but an extravaganza: a documentary revue, in the manner of *Forty Years On*, mocking our attitudes to the healing arts by juxtaposing parody with reality. For my taste, it's a finer show of fireworks than Alan Bennett's — sharper, truer, funnier, even more theatrical. The National Theatre obviously has its biggest sucess since *Rosencrantz and Guildenstern Are Dead.*

Greatly as I admired *Joe Egg* . . . the vein of parodic fantasy . . . spilled over in cartoon intrusion of [Bri's] comic comforters, upsetting the tightrope poise of the play's tone. *The National Health*, for all its pleasures, comes from this lower drawer of Nichols's talent. Penetratingly comic and intelligent, endlessly diverting, it lacks shape because it lacks certainty about its own point.

On the one hand Nichols wants to expose the sentimentality of our pretence that medicine is anything but a threadbare civic carpet on the path to the tomb. On the other he can't bear the harsh medical humour which recognizes hospitals as cadaver factories.

It's the quarrel between Bri and Sheila in *Joe Egg*, still unconcluded.

Perhaps one can only present the paradox, as he does, but by evading a clear statement of it in jokiness he robs his play of a spine. Still, he's gathered up in his bleak microcosm more of modern Britain . . . than we've seen in the theatre since Osborne's *Entertainer*, and Michael Blakemore's stunning production confirms . . . that he's the liveliest rising director on the scene.

Ronald Bryden, *The Observer*, 19 Oct. 1969

The play's intricate web of changing relationships . . . unfolds with an impartiality and compassion that can be compared only with Chekhov.

Irving Wardle, *The Times*, 20 Jan. 1971

On the New York production

The National Health is in poor condition, and although it was a major success in London, it is a transplant that doesn't function.

Pat Collins, WCBS TV 2, 10 Oct. 1974

Sure, it will make you laugh, and it may make you want to cry. A fine play.

Leonard Probst, NBC, 10 Oct. 1974

We soon find that *The National Health* comprises a number of issues, including national health services, racism, euthanasia, abortion, and capital punishment. The commentary is always oblique, telling us about the patients and their times.

Television is the patients' only contact with the outside world. Through a surrealistic transition, the television is used to describe what is going on between the doctors and nurses. . . . The soap-opera romance . . . suggests that most of life's niceties turn into soap when seen from a hospital bed.

Christopher Sharp, *Women's Wear Daily*, 11 Oct. 1974

One of the best plays of the season. It is a flawed work of pure genius, and should be seen by anyone with an interest in the contemporary theatre.

The National Health is another exploration into the queasily danger-ous area of bad taste. Mr. Nichols finds cancer a subject for laughter, but he also finds all the ills affecting us, from the new-born baby to the senile child awaiting death, a matter of compassion and concern. As a playwright he offers us savage and irresistible laughter.

Mr. Nichols is writing here on many levels. He is expressing with a wry, dry wit, the ridiculous universality of human life and human ills. He achieves this, in part, through the character of Barnet, who is a hospital orderly often playing a vaudeville clown. Barnet makes asides, he steps away from the play's naturalistic background, yet he also points out the reality of life and death. . . . He is a death figure, in a white coat, who talks with the familiarity of a nightclub comic. He is where we are going.

Clive Barnes,
New York Times, 11 Oct. 1974

There are a number of patients whose only characterization is what illness each has and what part of British society each represents, this being an exercise in social and philosophical relevance. They are never individuals and Nichols has given them no story other than living or dying.

Martin Gottfried,
New York Post, 11 Oct. 1974

It is a play in which the disgustingness of our failed mortality — the bedpans equally with the senile loss of reason — is transformed and rendered acceptable. Mr. Nichols implies that the price we pay for living is almost intolerably high, but 'almost' is the word he emphasizes and celebrates.

Brendan Gill, *The New Yorker*, 21 Oct. 1974

The play is very well written, with the special English talent for characterization of the humble and the down and out. In short, a good play.

Harold Clurman, *The Nation*, 2 Nov. 1974

On the film version

In the cinema . . . although the screenplay is by Peter Nichols himself, the larger concerns all but disappear.

Moreover, the *Nurse Norton* parody side is overloaded, rather poorly observed, and just not very funny. It lacks stylistic precision as well as the wild exuberance that was achieved on the stage.

The Times, 9 Mar. 1973

On the TV screening of the film

What helps to keep this from collapsing into *Carry on Nurse II* is the anger that enables Nichols to keep his subject — as opposed to this particular emergency ward — in focus, and which emerges in some wonderful moments of comic bile.

Richard Combs,
The Listener, 29 Nov. 1990

Forget-Me-Not Lane

A play in two acts.
First production: Greenwich Th., 1 Apr. 1971, trans. Apollo Th., London, 28 Apr. 1971 (dir. Michael Blakemore; with Anton Rodgers as Frank, Michael Bates as Charles, Ian Gelder as Young Frank, Joan Hickson as Amy, Malcolm McFee as Ivor, Eddie Molloy as Mr. Magic, Stephanie Lawrence as Miss Nineteen-Forty, Priscilla Morgan as Ursula, and Sandra Payne as Young Ursula).
Television production: BBC TV, 5 Nov. 1975 (dir. Alan Bridges; with Albert Finney as Frank, Bill Fraser as Charles, and Gemma Jones as Ursula).
Revived: Greenwich Th., March, 1990 (dir. Nichols; with Philip Jackson as Frank, Matthew Lloyd Davies as Young Frank, Bryan Pringle as Charles, Dilys Watling as Ursula, Catrin Menna as Young Ursula, and Charles Pemberton as Mr. Magic).
First American production: Long Wharf Th., New Haven, trans. Mark Taper Forum, Los Angeles (dir. Arvin Brown). This production was later transmitted by WNET TV.
Published: Faber, 1971; *Plays: One*.

37

Packing his suitcase in the present, Frank is confronted by the past: the adolescent struggle to grow up intellectually and sexually within the confines of a household in which the sad, absurd aspirations of the puritanical father are deflated by the banal realities accepted by the mother.

Though the theme was gloomy and pessimistic, the play kept smiling through. . . . It worked better on the stage than anything of mine before or since. *Forget-Me-Not Lane* is still my favourite, the most personal and satisfying, though it has had only moderate success since the first magical performances at Greenwich. Probably no other stage has suited it as well as the one it was written for.

Nichols, *Plays: One* (1987), p. 3-4.

Mr Nichols's profound compassion gets an immediate response from his audience and his uncannily accurate eye for the minutiae of family life and for the remembered absurdities of wartime England cause continuous waves of laughter. It is the laughter of recognition, and it is deep and true.

Frank Marcus,
Sunday Telegraph, Apr. 1971

On Wednesday, BBC 2 devoted not far short of two hours to *Forget-Me-Not Lane*. . . . But there was almost no narrative interest, only discourse. Civilized discourse, certainly, bantering, all quite pleasant for half an hour, and then dull, and, finally, very dull indeed.

The playwright's central problem was self-engendered. He had sketched for us, in the present, Frank . . . a man of 40, his wife Ursula . . . his three children, but then insisted on . . . flashbacks to the period of the last war, when Frank and Ursula had been growing up. Or, in Frank's case, not growing up. . . . The man had been emotionally stunted but it was tiring to dwell on what had stunted him all those years ago, when he was dithering here and now.

Parent trouble, of course. Frank had a father to hate, an old-timer, broader of beam than of mind, crusty with his wife and son, a Dickensian would-have-been. There was life in him.

D. Pryce-Jones,
The Listener, 13 Nov. 1975

On Nichols's own production, 1990

Nichols treats the situation with a tetchy lyricism; a unique blend of love, pity, exasperation and grief-stricken contempt. We ought to come away feeling that in the end poor old Charles has more worth and substance than his endlessly fantasizing son; but Nichols's own production comes between us and his play. The action lacks the lethal snappiness of the writing. . . .

John Peter, Sunday Times, 25 Mar. 1990

Bare breasted girls and lecherous pederasts live on stage no longer thrill, exposing the flimsiness of this reminiscence exercise. The emotional core could be intriguing: the disintegration of dreary Frank's relationship with his parents as he attempts to fulfil his post-war aspirations, and liberate mind and body from their lower middle-class-anxieties.

Carl Miller, City Limits, 23 March 1990

We are more aware of the play's lack of narrative . . . and the passage of time has also pointed up its indifference and hostility to women (somewhat softened, however, in the slightly rewritten version).

Rhoda Koenig, Punch, 30 March 1990

In 1970 the sight and sound of a grown man ranting at his parents for what they made him or indulging in adolescent speculation about his wife's past as a teenage temptress might have seemed liberating. Now Frank's pompous confessions sound plain embarrassing.

John Morrish, Time Out, 28 Mar. 1990

A play about unexorcised ghosts. Middle-aged selves look back with a little shiver at young selves; the family dramas of the 1940s rise up to haunt 1970. . . . Man hands on misery to man.

But the play is a comedy too. Partly a comedy of adolescence; partly the comedy of Dad, who has to be fought against, worried over, and ultimately forgiven. . . .

But the play retains an essential core of emotional truth. You wince, you recognize, you sympathize, you smile.

Perhaps it would have been better if the production itself hadn't played up the pain so explicitly, if it had given freer rein to the elements of fantasy and burlesque.

John Gross,
Sunday Telegraph, 25 Mar. 1990

The piece is like an expanded Larkin poem, with young Frank (Nichols's alter ego) re-enacting his first sexual experiments under the withering scrutiny of his middle-aged self. . . .

Memory, as Nichols presents it, is Pandora's box. Open it, and you lose control of the contents. Novelists know all about this. To show it on stage required a new technique, which Nichols supplied by combining direct narration with remembered scenes, all located in a continuous psychological present. For audiences primed on the flashback, it came as a stunning insight when the remembered characters started talking back to the hero — 'I'm part of your mental landscape for ever, duckie' — until he is screaming at them to leave him alone.

Since then the technique has been exploited by other writers and it has less than its original impact in the revival. . . . The fault, though, is in the production, not in the writing, though some odd things have happened to the text, such as the cutting of an early exchange establishing that Frank has left his wife, Ursula.

Irving Wardle,
Independent on Sunday, 25 Mar. 1990

This dramatic conceit is a perfect way of illustrating the fact that we only understand people when it is too late to be of any use.

Becoming our fathers may help us forgive them, but there is a less lovely corollary to this which says that forgiving our fathers is a hypocritical way of being soft on ourselves and on what we have become. *Forget-Me-Not Lane* could afford to be much more stringent on this point.

Paul Taylor,
The Independent, 22 Mar. 1990

Forget-Me-Not Lane remains one of Mr. Nichols's best plays. But, in highlighting its emotional truth at the expense of its raffish brio, Mr. Nichols the director conscientiously excavates the pain instead of

allowing it to emerge through the laughter. One concludes that writers
are not automatically the best directors of their own work.

Michael Billington, *The Guardian*, 21 Mar. 1990

A meticulous, minutely detailed, loving mockery of a nation and a
family in decline, the play is, in the end, about a man discovering that he
was too young ever to deal with his parents and now too old to cope
with his children.

Sheridan Morley,
Herald Tribune, 28 Mar. 1990

The play contains elements of music hall, farce . . . and fantasy. . . . [It] . . .
remains a fine study of the inevitable struggle between generations.

Annalen McAfee,
Evening Standard, 20 Mar. 1990

Neither Up Nor Down

A sketch.
First production: Almost Free Theatre, Soho, 28 Jan. 1972 (dir. Ed
    Berman).
Published: Plays: One (1987).

*A married couple try to revive their flagging sexuality by
following the illustrated instructions in a sex manual.*

Tynan has been persuading me to write a turn for *Oh, Calcutta!* . . .
Spent a day writing what seemed to Thelma and me a funny five
minutes and gave it to Ken next morning. He later rang to say he found
it funny but would have to show it to Clifford Williams, the show's
director, when he came back from New York. This morning, weeks later,
receive a nasty little note from Williams saying the sketch is too much
like another in the show. . . .

Nichols, *Plays: One* (1987), p. 147

Beasts of England

Anthology of readings for the stage, from the works of George Orwell.
Performance: planned at National Theatre, 1973, prevented by Orwell's
   widow.

I'm greatly influenced by Orwell. In fact, I did a thing on Orwell for the
National when Tynan and Olivier were still running it, which wasn't
anything to do with coming up to 1984; it was long before that. But they
wanted to do a platform production, a four acter or five acter to
take round on tour. . . . I just read all of Orwell and selected pieces
which told his life story. Mrs. Orwell jumped on it and said, 'Oh I won't
allow this.'

> Nichols, in conversation with Andrew Parkin, May 1987

Chez Nous

A play in two acts.
First performance: Globe Th., London, 6 Feb. 1974 (dir. Robert
   Chetwyn; with Albert Finney as Phil, Denholm Elliott as Dick,
   Geraldine McEwan as Diana, Pat Heywood as Liz, Denis Carey as
   Gunga Din, Beth Porter as Zoe, and Glenn Beck as Burt).
First New York production: Manhattan Theatre Club, Nov. 1977
   (dir. Lynne Meadow; with Sam Waterston as Phil, John Tillinger as
   Dick, Christina Pickles as Diana, and Barbara Caruso as Liz).
Published: Faber, 1974; *Plays: One* (1987); *Plays: Two.*

*Mr. Nichols puts a foot into Nabokov Country to tell the story of
a successful paediatrician and his wife who have moved from
London to the South of France and discover that one of their
oldest and closest friends, a semi-successful architect, is the
father of the illegitimate infant grandson — their daughter, Jane,
having been thirteen years old at the time of conception. . . . The
action is mostly a matter of conversations and confidences
among the four . . . and by the time the evening is over we know
all about their private griefs and yearnings. Yet Mr. Nichols
maintains a comic tone throughout. . . . Also by the time the*

*evening is over, we realize that the status is, and will remain,
quo, for a theme of the play is the unbreakability, the perma-
nence, of these fragile-seeming marriages.*
Edith Oliver, *The New Yorker*, 21 Nov. 1977

As it was being played [a few days before opening night] Dick ended the
play by ending his marriage, going off to his room to write her a farewell
note. It was bad stagecraft and untrue to the man.

I had written a dozen endings already and one of these was now
taken up by Michael Medwin. It was his refinement of my thought that
showed me what I must do. Next day I wrote what now stands and when
Denholm Elliott played this version . . . it was certainly an improvement
but not a solution.
Nichols, *Plays: One* (1987), p.162-3

It may seem a back-handed compliment to describe Nichols's work as
the present high-water mark of middle-class society drama, and
who knows whether it will strike future spectators as provincial as
The Second Mrs. Tanqueray now seems to us. But, for the time being,
here is an artist who has thought his subject through to a hard-won
comic detachment, and who treats story telling as a moral action. Our
theatre has no more satisfying experience to offer.

But Nichols is after bigger game than trivial class absurdities; and he
first shows his hand while Dick is smugly showing off the family
snapshots, which reveal that his wife could not have given birth to the
family's new baby. There follow two surprises which, with apologies, I
must disclose: first that this is the child of Liz's fourteen-year-old
daughter, and secondly that its father was friendly old Phil. It is a
situation that puts all the characters' values to the dramatic test. . . .

An extraordinary concluding image, which strikes me as one of the
great endings of modern drama.
Irving Wardle, *Sunday Times*, 7 Feb. 1974

The wily Peter Nichols has grasped the fact that the constraints of
convention can be turned to excellent subversive use. . . . We laugh, but
the evening becomes a therapeutic purgation.
Frank Marcus, *Sunday Telegraph*, 10 Feb. 1974

43

It is the best new play in London and the best its author has written.

The association of these two fortyish married couples stretches back to their single days. . . . The only significant blemish on Robert Chetwyn's production is that it is sometimes difficult to accept this fact. . . . Dick is a paediatrician who has struck it rich with a book which someone has providentially persuaded him to entitle *The Nubile Baby*. . . . He knows he should despise money and fame but he enjoys the attention, having always resented his own bashfulness. In particular he resents the fact that his wife is the only woman he has had. . . . So in *The Nubile Baby* he rails against conventional sexual restraints and, of course, against the family. Which is ironic, since not only is his wife family personified, but they have three children of their own.

Only they have two. Their new baby son is actually their grandson begotten on their fourteen-year-old daughter (first surprise) by old pal and present guest, Phil (second surprise). . . .

A battle for possession of the baby . . . comes to dominate the play. Given something to fight for, Albert Finney's tousled performance takes on extraordinary strength; this is his definitive roaring boy.

But it is Dick on whom the play finally closes in; for funnier, for sadder, Mr. Nichols has here developed and enriched the themes of loneliness and aching regret which he adumbrated in *Forget-Me-Not Lane* and *A Day in the Death of Joe Egg*. Denholm Elliott gives him occasional surges of joy . . . rising from a sea of *angst*: the resigned agony of a man who has reached the middle of his life and the end of his tether simultaneously.

At least two scenes should make the history books: a terminal silent solo by Mr. Elliott, and a central quartet of recrimination which plays like classic comedy. . . . Formally this is his least obviously experimental play, and his most successful.

Robert Cushman, *The Observer*, 10 Feb. 1974

The Freeway

A play in two acts.

First production: National Theatre Company at the Old Vic, 1 Oct. 1974 (dir. Jonathan Miller; with Paul Rogers as Les, Irene Handl as May, Lionel Murton as Wally, Joan Hickson as Evelyn, Graham Crowden as James, Rachel Kempson as Nancy, Pip Miller as Grant, Doran Godwin as Tracy, Antony Brown as Cox, Sara Van Beers as Payne, Veronica Sowerby as Nurse, and Mark Dignam as Barry).

Radio version: broadcast in 1991.

Published: Faber, 1975; *Play: One* (1991).

I suspect Nichols is the first dramatist to make a traffic jam the scene of a full-length play, and the Cherokee dormobile with the lavatory that leaks into the drinking water system must surely be the first internal combustion engine to star in a play at the National Theatre. Nichols presents us with a grey and unpleasant land, governed by a party that has achieved power by promising a car for every family and road space for every car.... But anti-social forces are at work: some say it is the reactionary anti-motorists, others that it is members of the Wreckers' Union; either way, traffic has ground to a halt. Nichols portrays the bestiality of an acquisitive society mainly through comic means.

Charles Lewsen, *The Times*, 2 Oct. 1974

The trouble is that although Mr. Nichols may well be saying important things, which the players enunciate with their customary *éclat*, he puts them in such a way that they seem rather uninteresting. The characters' relationships with each other remain as static as the stranded cars.

Harold Hobson, *Sunday Times*, 6 Oct. 1974

Early on in the present piece someone speaks of 'the Free Way,' tentatively breaking up the syllables as if testing them for their weight-bearing capacity. By the end of the evening the metaphor is full-blown. . . .

The metaphor is neater than that of *The National Health* and I . . . found it reasonably convincing. It is not, though, dramatically interesting. There is no passion behind Mr. Nichols's version of the future, no real point of view, and not even very much indignation: just a generalized cynicism.

Stretches of *The Freeway* are very funny, but it keeps running into road blocks. Some of these are the fault of the production; for its realization the text demands clean technical virtuosity, the quality in which Jonathan Miller as a director is most notably deficient.

Robert Cushman, *The Observer*, 6 Oct. 1974

The motoring metaphors come naturally, as the setting is a traffic jam stretching 100 miles and lasting three days and nights.

This device has been used before, notably in films by Godard and Tati and in a television play [*The Gorge*] by Peter Nichols himself, but

45

this does not invalidate it as a symbol. . . . Schematically, as in a late Shavian *pièce à thèse*, one would expect the characters to be the mouthpieces of conflicting points of view, arguing their cases with clarity and penetrating insight. But, inexplicably, Mr. Nichols tries to resolve his dilemma in terms of naturalistic domestic comedy: two mutually exclusive forms of drama forced into the same frame. He has shed his customary ploys — direct address to the audience and interpolated fantasy sequences — in the very play that needs them.

Frank Marcus, *Sunday Telegraph*, 6 Oct. 1974

If plot is defined as characters changing in response to events, the events occurring because of the interaction of characters, then Mr. Nichols's *National Health* was a pretty static affair, too. There's nothing wrong with a play that's mainly concerned to anatomize a given situation and discuss the issues raised — provided, of course, it is all done with depth as well as breadth. But here *The Freeway* seems suspect. . . . We have . . . a cross-section of the concrete society. But there are cross-sections and cross-sections, and I think that Labour and Tory alike are entitled to feel mildly libelled by the types selected to represent them. . . .

Their cumulative efforts don't take the debate very far. We learn that individual self-indulgence can produce social misery; that labour tends to equate happiness with possessions, and that capital is only too glad to keep its power with the odd handout; that freedom, in short, may be slavery. But anyone who has read a little nineteenth-century history, or even heard a few economic discussions on *Panorama*, will want to see more slippery questions tackled. How, without real economic growth, can everybody in this country expect a reasonably secure life?

Benedict Nightingale, *New Statesman*, 11 Oct. 1974

This is a dramatist who has hitherto seemed possessed of as vivaciously original a comic talent as anyone presently operating in the theatre, and it is as surprising as it is dismaying to find that talent . . . foundering bleakly. . . .

In the little section of the jam presented on the stage, he offers us some stereotyped caricatures of the working class and of the aristocracy, and it is hard to say whether his patronizing view of the former or the quaint naivety that informs his disdain of the latter is the more painful. Neither, though, is quite so distressing as the fact that his F1 and the trouble that develops on it are a tortured metaphor for British democracy, class-ridden and acquisitive, careering along a freeway to

disaster. . . . This is a case in which one might agree with what he says
but oppose to the death his tedious way of saying it.

Kenneth Hurren, *The Spectator*, 12 Oct. 1974

There is something curiously detached and empty about the play. It
appears to lack passion; Nichols unearths some misgivings, but never
digs deeply.

Helen Dawson, *Plays and Players*, Nov. 1974

Although Peter Nichols is primarily intent on ridiculing the motor car as
a cult totem of success, he is also out to deride the affluent philosophy of
the masses, the callous exploitation of those vulgar tastes by cynical
politicians, the sheeplike docility of the millions when they are confronted by authority. The contrast between their plight and their insensitivity
to it is one of the play's most endearing and frightening ingredients.

Milton Shulman, *Evening Standard*, Oct. 1974

'After the failure of *The Freeway* . . . I went through a couple of bad
years. It stopped me in my tracks. I couldn't believe it. I thought I maybe
didn't know what critics and audiences wanted. I had this terrible suspicion at the back of my mind — something Waugh said of authors —
that I only had a couple of things to write about, and the rest was
professional trickery.'

A particular 'trick' for which Nichols has been admired is the use of
music hall and revue techniques in the treatment of taboo subjects. . . .
His skill lies in the elision of patter and numbers with plotting and
characterization.

Jim Hiley, 'Liberating Laughter',
Plays and Players, Mar. 1978, p.14.

See also:
Sheridan Morley, '*The Freeway* and Freedom Going Wrong',
   The Observer, 28 Sept. 1974, p. 11.
John Weightman, 'Metaphysical Voids: on Ayckbourn and Nichols',
   Encounter, Dec. 1974, p. 64-6.

Harding's Luck

An adaptation for Christmas of 'two time fantasies' by E. Nesbit.
First production: Greenwich Th., 26 Dec. 1974.

*On the first night, the mechanical scenery exploded and nervous
parents hustled their children to the exits, believing it was the
latest of a spate of IRA bombings. Few plays recover from
disastrous openings and this was no exception.*

Peter Nichols, *Plays: One* (1987), p. 293

Privates on Parade

A play with songs in two acts.
First production: Royal Shakespeare Company at Aldwych Th.,
London, 17 Feb. 1977 (music by Denis King; dir. Michael
Blakemore; with Denis Quilley as Terri Dennis, Nigel Hawthorne as
Major Flack, Ian Gelder as Private Steven Flowers, Joe Melia as
Corporal Len Bonny, David Daker as Sergeant-Major Reg
Drummond, Emma Williams as Sylvia Morgan, Ben Cross as Flight
Sergeant Kevin Cartwright, Tim Wylton as Lance-Corporal Charles
Bishop, Simon Jones as Leading Aircraftman Eric Young-Love,
Richard Rees as Lee, and John Venning as Cheng).
Revivals: Piccadilly Theatre, London, 2 Feb. 1978 (Michael
Blakemore's production; but with Shaun Curry as Sergeant-Major
Drummond, Neil McCaul as Flight Sergeant Cartwright, Cecil Cheng
as Lee, and Eiji Kusuhara as Cheng); Birmingham Repertory Th.,
Apr. 1988 (dir. Derek Nicholls; revised script by Nichols, with new
ending not in Faber or Methuen texts).
First American production: Long Wharf Th., New Haven, 6 June 1979
(dir. Arvin Brown; with Jim Dale as Terri Dennis and Robert Joy as
Private Flowers).
First New York production: Roundabout Th., 22 Aug. 1989 (dir. Larry
Carpenter; with Jim Dale as Terri Dennis, Simon Jones as Major
Flack, Jim Fyfe as Private Flowers, Ross Bickell as Corporal Bonny,
Gregory Jbara as Flight Sergeant Cartwright, Donald Burton as
Sergeant-Major Drummond, Donna Murphy as Sylvia Morgan,
Edward Hibbert as Leading Aircraftman Young-Love, John Curry as
Lance-Corporal Bishop, Tom Matsusaka as Lee, and Stephen Lee as
Cheng).

Film: released by Handmade Films, 1983 (script by Nichols; dir.
   Michael Blakemore; with original cast, except for John Cleese as
   Major Flack and Nicola Pagett as Sylvia Morgan).
Published: Faber 1977; *Plays: One* (1987); *Plays: Two.*

---

*National Serviceman Private Steven Flowers is initiated into
several new worlds – those of the military, of tropical Malaya, of
communist insurgency and political awareness, the theatrical
world of SADUSEA, and the world of adult sexuality, homo- and
heterosexual.*

I began reworking an old play about my airforce days to stop myself
brooding. There'd been a good few false starts over the years, including
one attempt at co-authorship with Charles Wood, but none had got
beyond the opening scenes. All that survived from these were the
opening chorus and the name of the entertainments company — Song
and Dance Unit South East Asia or SADUSEA. Looking up the precise
meaning of Sadducee, I found that he was a sceptical materialist,
member of a sect that denied the resurrection of the dead. . . . My first
cracks at it were out of Büchner, Brecht, *Schweik*, and *Oh! What a
Lovely War.* I never meant it to be a musical or even (as I still prefer to
call it) a play with songs, but soon realized that a show about a gang of
singers and dancers which had no songs would be a flightless bird.

Nichols, *Plays: One* (1987), p. 293

He [Michael Blakemore] had his chance to begin rehearsals without me
and, when I came back, the thing had taken on a life of its own. The
'play' suffered, the show won. The Chinese prompters, representing the
entire native population, had become mere supers and the balance
between East and West was lost. . . . There's usually one performance
from a production that stays in the memory and mine is of the last run-
through in the dingy rehearsal-room in Covent Garden when Trevor
Nunn and other brasshats came to see what the lads had put together. It
was also the last time the balance was right. After that, the costumes, the
orchestra, the lights, the settings, all allowed the song-and-dance to
dominate. I always enjoyed watching *Privates* but never knew how to
give the play back what the show had taken.
   The version here is my latest attempt to restore the balance. It
includes various changes from the first Aldwych production and later

49

ones from the revival at the Piccadilly, the only American showing at New Haven, and my screenplay for the feature film. An Andrews Sisters song, added for the film, is also retained. The 'new' ending of Sylvia's story is a return to the first version I ever wrote, which turns out to be the strongest and most true and was used in the film.

Nichols, *Plays: One* (1987), p. 295

It was with CSE [Combined Services Entertainments] that my education began. I read *The Ragged-Trousered Philanthropists* and Bernard Shaw's *Political What's What* and became a lifelong leftie. Stanley Baxter explained Existentialism and the rest of us nodded intelligently, lounging in our Chinese satin kimonos, smoking through cigarette holders. We even had a sub-culture — the world of queans (nineteenth-twentieth century Australian from OE cwene) with its own lingo and world-view. The early scenes in *Privates* showing Steven's initiation are a fair account of my own. The original for Terri Dennis, the drag-artiste, was Barri Chatt, a civilian dancer escaping the rigours of Attlee's Britain.

Twelve of us were in a revue called *At Your Service*. 'We're men of the service, We're at your service entertaining you!' we shouted in the opening number. . . . Kenneth Williams followed with imitations of Bette Davis, Nellie Wallace, and Felix Aylmer. . . . There was tap-dancing, magic, a torchlit choir singing 'Pedro the Fisherman', and a cod panto. We toured the island, mainland Malaya, and Hong Kong in search of an audience. . . . Five thousand Chinese guerrillas were preparing to create a state of emergency for over ten years, holding down ten times their number of British forces, as well as a hundred thousand police and home guard. The Communists learnt a hard lesson from their eventual defeat; the French and Americans presumably did not.

Nichols, 'Tropical Scandals', *The Times*, 7 Feb. 1978

As is usual in service comedies, the men are clowns and the officer an uncomprehending stooge. But this time the distinction is more than metaphorical, since we are concerned with an entertainments unit whose contribution to freedom is the production of — in every sense — camp concerts. Double-entendres are the Order of the Day, beginning with the title. . . . Denis Quilley, tempering his usual robust enthusiasm with a certain primness, storms gaily through impersonations of Marlene Dietrich, Vera Lynn, and Carmen Miranda before coming to rest as a surprisingly fleshly Noel Coward (actually he looks more like Donald

Sinden). . . . If you can mentally combine 'There Are Bad Times Just around the Corner' with 'Could You Please Oblige Us with a Bren Gun' you will have the right idea. Certainly the author and his composer (Denis King) have it, here and throughout; with so many of our playwrights attempting to turn themselves into lyricists, Mr. Nichols is ahead of the field . . . supreme, too, as a fashioner of one-liners, dead in character and dead funny.

The play is, however, very long and decidedly unwieldy. . . . The story comes in two interlocking sections. There is a love element, played with a nice mixture of passion and bewilderment by Emma Williams . . . and Ian Gelder, who impersonated the youthful Mr. Nichols in *Forget-Me-Not Lane* and is here, I imagine, continuing the biography. There is also a sinister bit concerning a villainous sergeant-major, a source of bafflement to author, actor, director, and me.

In theory, all these scenes are stylized — dramatic numbers in the concert-party to balance the musical ones — but the idea is scuppered by Mr. Nichols's frequent recourse to passages of extended naturalism. The framework vanishes, if not from the stage, then certainly from the audience's consciousness. I doubt its necessity anyway; the device, for all its fun, represents a step backwards for Mr. Nichols.

Robert Cushman, *The Observer*, 27 Feb. 1977

For once the word hilarious is the right one . . . but at the same time I must record the strong characterization from other members of Mr. Quilley's unit, not only by the C.O. — one of Mr. Nichols's most formidable father images — but also by the various sergeants and corporals. . . .

Anthony Curtis,
Drama, No. 124 (Spring 1977) p. 47

Behind all the high jinks, the larks, the quiddities of character, the jokes and the gags, Mr. Nichols is asking a question of vital importance. What has western civilization to offer in place of what is offered (or rather, what simple-minded people think is offered) by Communism?

The only man in the play who has any body of doctrine in him is the character whom the audience is most ready to ridicule, that is, Major Flack . . . a kindly but woefully conventional Christian. . . . When he makes his fundamentalist, public school little speeches the audience laughs at them. They represent a world universes away from our own permissive society. But an extraordinary thing happens. Nigel

51

Hawthorne plays the Major with such conviction that we begin to take him seriously. And at the end he has his moment of triumph, all the greater because he is not thinking of triumph, but of sincerity. The foulest-mouthed of the play's characters is killed, and the Major pronounces over him the last words of *The Pilgrim's Progress*. Nothing could be more ludicrously inappropriate than to say of this swearing product of the Birmingham slums that, when he came to the river, 'he passed over, and all the trumpets sounded for him on the other side'. But they do not seem ludicrous to the Major, and Mr. Hawthorne times and spaces Bunyan's simple, glorious words so magnificently that the crowded theatre, its jeering laughter . . . stilled, listens in an absolute silence.

Harold Hobson,
Drama, No. 125 (Summer 1977) p. 39-40

On the first American production

Jim Dale . . . is a grand and compelling reason for being at New Haven's Long Wharf Theatre at the present moment instead of wherever you happen to be.

Peter Nichols . . . has really scrambled three plays here — a sequel to *Oh! What a Lovely War*, a sequel to *The Boys in the Band*, and an indigenous British product of the past quarter-century that might be called *Britannia Rues the Waves*. This is a form of retroactive remorse for colonialist sins that one no longer possesses the power to commit.

T. E. Kalem, *Time*, 25 June, 1979

On the film

'Peter and I have pulled together what was originally a series of music hall sketches', explains Blakemore, 'by taking up one stray narrative thread that was just dangling there in the play. This is the story of the corrupt sergeant-major Reg Drummond, played by Michael Elphick. He's smuggling arms to the rebels and he now contrives to have the troupe go on tour so he can use it as a caravan for running the guns up country. The music sketches now make more sense. The tighter construct makes stronger the points that Peter wanted to make in the play. It is all much more shocking.'

Christopher Keats, 'How Privates Got Promotion',
The Guardian, 30 Aug. 1982.

What is notable about [the film] — and those who have seen the stage version could hardly doubt the fact — is Denis Quilley's performance as Acting Captain Terri Dennis. . . . This is an extended cameo in a million, as good as that of either of the leading couples in *Cage aux Folles* but with a great deal more depth, since this . . . so movingly portrays the agony behind the camp ecstasy.

Yet it is still not a good film, chiefly because it falls . . . between the particular dimensions of theatre and cinema.

Its real fault, however, is that the adaptation simply does not work as a screen entity. Even so, I wouldn't put you off it. Nichols's play is simply too good to be beaten, and the performances are a lasting pleasure even within a botched framework.

Derek Malcolm, *The Guardian*, 27 Jan. 1983

Within minutes Peter Nichols's tight [film] script, based on his 1977 play, has put Monty Python nuttiness into a straitjacket. In lyrics and wit he calls up the spirit of Noel Coward. We get a helping of *MASH*. *Carry On* carries on. It's *The Boy Friend* in drag, *Dad's Army* in tropical shorts, and the whole book of age-old army gags thrown at us.

These are not comparisons, invidious, critics for the use of, but a selection of the flavours which the film's rich texture releases with a nostalgia that's often close to heartache. . . . It's also triumphantly itself, a flight of bravura that brings theatre into the movie-house with operatic aplomb. . . .

But behind all these games — the joker in the package — lies a cruel plot . . . which spews violence at intervals, timed nicely, almost drowning us in the guilt of our laughter. The humour then has the extra hilarity of the not really funny, the horror behind things. But we're soon back to base: 'one film, tragi-comic, finely turned out, audiences for the delight of.'

David Hughes, *The Times*, 30 Jan. 1983

On the Birmingham revival

This new production, on Birmingham's cavernous stage, draws on material from the Faber and Samuel French editions . . . as well as the Methuen edition of the collected plays (1987); and there are changes even from this latest text. . . .

Through his parodies of popular songs of the period, and even more their placing after scenes of carnage and folly, Nichols mounts an attack on the old Imperial and Church Parade mystique that is blistering while it entertains. It is a high-wire act in which Nichols has always been a master.

This definitive version replaces the young-love ending with the quasi-heroic act of the outrageously camp, fundamentally decent Captain Terri Dennis, in marrying the pregnant Eurasian girl after she is abandoned by her lover. It is hard to understand how the alternative could ever have been preferred. Along with this, the whole show (director Derek Nicholls) is sourer and less glam.

Jeremy Kingston, *The Times*, 22 Apr. 1988

On the first New York production

Although hardly inaccessible to American audiences, the humour is . . . decidedly British in flavour and content. 'We are brought up on rude comedy', Mr. Dale [Terri Dennis] points out during an interview. . . .

The actor is himself a veteran of pantomime theatre — that very popular and peculiarly British entertainment combining familiar nursery stories with contemporary social comedy and raucous burlesque humour — and can trace its antecedents to commedia dell'arte and ancient Roman mime plays. In its performance tradition of male comedians cavorting in female roles, Mr. Dale also found a major source of inspiration for Terri Dennis's flashy impersonations in *Privates on Parade* of Marlene Dietrich, Carmen Miranda, and Vera Lynn.

To Mr. Nichols, the panto Dame has another layer — as 'a surrogate Queen, a parody of our own Queen' — which adds a slightly subversive tinge to her cartoonish colors.

Marilyn Stasio, *New York Times*, 20 Aug. 1989

Despite its occasional suggestions of seriousness, the play is outranked by other works by the author, beginning with *Joe Egg* and *Forget-Me-Not-Lane*. . . . As a satiric commentary on colonialism, *Privates on Parade* is shadowed by Caryl Churchill's *Cloud Nine*.

In its favour, it has an easygoing spontaneity. . . . The score . . . is a nostalgic pastiche of a period when Hollywood ruled Britannia.

Mel Gussow, *New York Times*, 23 Aug. 1989

For however long we've been dutifully going to the theatre, hoping and hoping (and failing) to see the real thing, we recognize it at once when it appears. That unmistakable thrill can currently be had at the Roundabout Theatre's revival of the 1977 play/musical by Peter Nichols.

In a monologue halfway through the first act, Mr. Dale shows us the ache that fuels Terri's constantly convivial chatter.

If in its colonies Britain is waging a war for the souls of the natives, *Privates on Parade* delineates how a country also wages war for the souls of its young men. . . .

Laurie Winer,
Wall Street Journal, 1 Sept. 1989

If it weren't for Nichols's evident desire to say something serious about war, English militarism, and the twilight of empire, *Privates on Parade* would be an altogether jolly evening in the theatre.

Instead of intensifying the action, as happens with Brecht, his evident model, Nichols's musical interludes obfuscate it. Play an audience old music, and even if your words and actions parody it brutally, they'll tune out the verbal comment and take the number as an affectionate gesture of nostalgia.

Once you carve your way past the cleverness, it's very hard to tell what Nichols thinks of the old British Empire and its way of life.

Some people marvel at his glib ingenuity; with me it always leaves an icky aftertaste, of pain fielded rather than faced, issues manipulated rather than dealt with.

Michael Feingold, *Village Voice*, 5 Sept. 1989

Dale is deliriously funny and endearing, walking the tightrope between character and caricature as surely as he trod a real highwire in *Barnum.* . . . With meticulous and inventive direction by Larry Carpenter and choreography by Daniel Pelzig, the show is blissful fun.

Holly Hill, *The Times*, London, 6 Sept. 1989

As in all his other plays, the form of *Privates* crept up on him, and he had anyway been working at the play on and off for fifteen years . . . and the non-musical sequences have been modified still further for the revival at the Piccadilly. . . . Nichols has made a bitter-sweet concoction, but audiences appear to him only to swallow the sweet parts.

Jim Hiley, 'Liberating Laughter',
Plays and Players, Mar. 1978, p. 15.

See also:
'Profile' of Peter Nichols, *Observer Colour Magazine*, 20 Feb. 1977.
John Russell Brown, *Short Guide to Modern British Drama*, p. 73-4.

Born in the Gardens

A play in two acts.

First production: Bristol Old Vic Company, Theatre Royal, Bristol,
29 Aug. 1979 (dir. Nichols; with Beryl Reid as Maud, Barry Foster
as Mo, Peter Bowles as Hedley, and Jennie Linden as Queenie).

First London production: Globe Th., 23 Jan. 1980 (dir. Clifford
Williams; with Jan Waters as Queenie).

Television production: BBC 1, 23 Aug. 1986 (dir. Robert Chetwyn; with
Constance Chapman as Maud, Barry Foster as Morris, Sheila Gish as
Queenie, and John Stride as Hedley).

Published: Faber, 1980; *Plays: Two*.

*Maud and her son Mo, an antiquarian bookseller and also a
traditional jazz fan, live in a mock-Tudor Victorian house in
Bristol. Maud's other children, Hedley, a Labour MP, and
Queenie, who lives in the USA, come home for a visit, because
of their father's death. Mo tolerates Maud's eccentricities,
but Hedley and Queenie attempt to improve their way of life by
suggesting Maud live in a modern 'duplex' in London and Mo
join Queenie in California. Both prefer their niche in Bristol,
Mo with his jazz, Maud talking back to her TV set and obsessed
with 'mites' that she thinks infest the house and even her
handbag.*

My theme is an argument for captivity, a blow against freedom, which
we can have too much of.

Nichols, quoted by Robert Ottaway,
'A Day in the Life of Peter Nichols', *Radio Times*, 23-29 Aug. 1986

Somewhere in this play of calculated eccentricity, Peter Nichols is
saying that life in the cage may offer more satisfaction than the illusion
of liberty or the freedom of choice.

By inserting an ironical attack on the British theatre, on characters who line up in plotless plays and make jokes that reflect on the state of Britain, he makes sure that his plotless play will also be seen to have its broader meaning.

The play . . . was first made public last autumn at the Bristol Old Vic, and has been reshaped by the new director, Clifford Williams, for the West End. It has one quality which I can recommend with pleasure, and that is the performance of Barry Foster as Mo.

Ned Chaillet, *The Times*, 24 Jan. 1980

Born in the Gardens is, as its author wryly acknowledges *en route*, a state-of-England play. When done last year at the Bristol Old Vic it was also a state-of-Bristol play, and this was the aspect on which the local audience seized most enthusiastically and infectiously. For its London transfer the piece has . . . been trimmed of many of these references, but the unfortunate result has been to leave both play and audience in limbo. . . .

I am less sure than everyone else seems to be that Mr. Nichols approves of his characters' obstinate desire to be left to a similar fate [captivity in a rut]; Hedley . . . seems to me a character drawn with both sympathy and wit. But the conclusion is long foregone and this . . . weighs the play down; it has to subsist on Maud's eccentricities. . . . Beryl Reid runs them for all they are worth. . . . Barry Foster, in an unusual role for him, and Peter Bowles, in a usual one, are, as before, excellent.

Robert Cushman, *The Observer*, 27 Jan. 1980

Three of the characters, the two sons and the malapropism-prone mother, are splendid Nichols grotesques. . . . The trouble arises with the fourth character, [Queenie] the Californianized daughter. . . . The reading of the part is undoubtedly superficial — we keep being told how anguished and screwed-up she is, but all we actually see for most of the play is a successfully, brainlessly liberated Ali MacGraw type of heroine — yet given the lines the woman has to speak in what I imagine we are supposed to take as unconvincing praise of her new life, I fail to see how any actress could make much more of her. This is sad, because elsewhere in the play, when Nichols is good he is very good indeed, and it is a thousand pities this one weak element throws all the rest off balance.

John Russell Taylor, *Drama*, No. 136 (Apr. 1980), p. 46

Queenie brings an outsider's eye to her native land, and likes nothing that she sees. . . . Queenie is played for all the sharpness she's worth by Jan Waters, who carries the tan becomingly as well.

Oddly, Nichols ends his first act with Queenie making a phone call without the realist prop: a cross between mime and monologue; and the second act begins with Hedley doing likewise. It is not, of course, the first time that Nichols has tried this degree of confrontation between character and audience, but it is a device that sits awkwardly in the context of *Born in the Gardens*, conveying little that could not have been brought out, if it needed to be brought out at all, in the otherwise admirable flow of dialogue. Bowles and Jan Waters, however, make the most of the showy acting opportunities these occasions afford them.

Nichols comes as near as dammit to being disarming . . . when he has one of his characters make a protest against the West End stage and the very type of play he is, so expertly, purveying. Since much of what he has to put across is dark, not to say pessimistic, I should . . . stress . . . that the tone . . . is nearly always funny, and at its best quite engagingly wry.

Gordon Gow,
Plays and Players, Feb. 1980, p. 28

On the television version

Dad is dead, and with varying degrees of covert or frank relief the family gathers in Bristol, more aware of the opportunities for change the demise of the old reprobate has presented than interested in lamentations.

The idea of reform, re-birth, opportunity, brings out in the stranded couple [Maud and Mo] a sly apathy, more than equal to the frenetic opportunism of the two visitors [Hedley and Queenie].

It is tempting to see in this a metaphor for derelict, dotty England. . . . But if it is a metaphor for England marooned, then we are being invited to join the castaways, since all our sympathy is directed towards the dotty ones.

Queenie is presented as in search of nothing much more than personal comfort and gratification of appetite; Hedley's faith in modernism and will to do good are demonstrated as hopelessly blind to real human needs. This pair go scurrying off . . . and leave us a few more cosy, comical moments with the wily ones, during which they reaffirm their commitment to their style of life. Eccentric old ladies are beloved of English cinema and theatre, and at times the play — opened out a little from the stage version — makes us feel back in the days of Ealing Studios, at a rather higher level of human description.

Peter Nichols's play is an illustration of Philip Larkin's 'They fuck you up, your mum and dad . . .' and the most impaired of the trio is Hedley.

Peter Lennon, *The Listener*, 20 Aug. 1986

Passion Play

A play in two acts.

First performance: Royal Shakespeare Company, Aldwych Th., London, 13 Jan. 1981 (dir. Mike Ockrent; with Billie Whitelaw as Eleanor, Priscilla Morgan as Agnes, Eileen Atkins as Nell, Benjamin Whitrow as James, Anton Rodgers as Jim, and Louise Jameson as Kate).

Revived: Haymarket Th., Leicester, 8 Mar. 1984, trans. Wyndham's Th., London, 18 Apr. 1984 (dir. Mike Ockrent; with Leslie Phillips as James, Barry Foster as Jim, Judy Parfitt as Eleanor, Zena Walker as Nell, Patricia Heneghan as Agnes, and Heather Wright as Kate).

First New York production: retitled *Passion*, Longacre Th., 15 May 1983 (dir. Marshall W. Mason; with Frank Langella as Jim, Bob Gunton as James, Cathryn Damon as Eleanor, E. Katherine Kerr as Nell, Stephanie Gordon as Agnes, and Roxanne Hart as Kate).

Published: Methuen, 1981; *Plays: Two.*

Eleanor and James are a married couple whose friend Albert has died, leaving a young widow, Kate. Kate begins an affair with James, provoking the appearance of his inner self, Jim. Agnes alerts Eleanor to James's adultery, provoking the appearance of Eleanor's inner self, Nell. These alter egos, clever deception in the plotting, and the use of significant bursts of music serve to deepen the interest of the sexual triangle. The pain of a broken marriage makes the wife suicidal. There are two possible endings: Nell leaves and Eleanor stays, or vice-versa.

Differences in casting in various productions made me realize that [Eleanor's and Nell's] roles could be swapped . . . and ELEANOR could leave while NELL stays, the point being that where the wives have

learned from and been changed by the events in the play, the husbands
have not. It may, in fact, be played either way.

Nichols, note to third revised edition,
Methuen, 1985

Passion Play makes my first serious use of music — all of it choral and
Christian, from Bach, Handel, Beethoven, and Verdi. The sounds made
by choirs are among the most sublime of all, the nearest I come to a
religious experience.

Nichols, quoted in programme note to the 1984 revival

The cast have been working on it under the provisional title *Passion
Play*. . . . It is permissible to reveal only that the play concerns a
menopausal marriage, one which is, says its author, 'anything but pure;
marriage is about ownership and parenthood and sickness and joint
accounts and being an open book' — which, one gathers, is where the
trouble starts.

Sheridan Morley, 'Billie Whitelaw: a Reckless Faith',
The Times Saturday Review, 10 Jan. 1981

I was once offered *Chez Nous* but I couldn't do that, and now that I am
rehearsing a Nichols script I find it the hardest thing I've done since
Beckett. Far tougher than *The Greeks*, largely because no single line
seems to follow on from any other single line.

Billie Whitelaw, quoted by Sheridan Morley, as above

Adultery may be the most popular theme in western drama, but there are
few plays that do justice to it, for the obvious reason that what goes on
in the secrecy of the partners' heads is far more dramatic than anything
they say, or for that matter do, to each other. Peter Nichols, having
observed this familiar obstacle, has characteristically found a technical
solution for it; an idea so simple and so comically fertile that it is
amazing that nobody to my knowledge has used it before. . . .

Kate, a husband-snatcher younger than James's daughter . . . propo-
sitions him over a restaurant table and gets her tongue down his throat
by the end of the meal. Passive and non-committal until now, the

sexually timid James omits to mention this amusing little adventure to his wife — at which point James B, his alter ego, bursts frantically on the scene to make sure he gets his story right. With the onset of lies the character splits in two, and the comedy begins.

In due course, Eleanor also acquires an Eleanor B. . . . James composes a compromising letter in the ground floor living room while a meddlesome family friend on the upper level hands it to Eleanor, who promptly splits in two.

With two characters, and two alter egos, the possible range of permutations is vast, and Nichols exploits them with a wonderful command of contrast, surprise, and observation of the revved-up thought-processes involved in weaving the tangled web.

Music is another powerful element in the production. . . . One of the meanest details . . . is the sight of James, radio in hand, informing Kate that he must get home as his wife's concert has just got around to the Agnus Dei, but that he will be available when she is otherwise engaged with the St. Matthew Passion and Mozart Requiem.

Nothing in the play carries a more potent charge of the pain, humiliation, and sadly retentive affections of this dismal subject, after all the lies are discovered, than the spectacle of the erring husband attempting to regain his wife's trust with a bungled groping assault on the stairs, to the immeasurably desolate accompaniment of Mozart's last work.

That concludes the first act, and the play could have stopped there. The second act has nothing like the same certainty of intention. In it, Nichols picks up his title pun and sets out to expand its religious implications. In this way, his earlier plays have regularly enriched small private experiences into works for the community.

But this time, although he carefully sets the scene by involving a pair of atheists in great devotional music and the restoration of religious paintings, the metaphor refuses to grow. . . . The worst one can say is that Nichols has written a small play, when one was hoping for a big one.

Irving Wardle, *The Times*, 15 Jan. 1981

The falling away of religious sanctions has, in a puzzling way, enriched rather than destroyed the subject [of adultery]. . . . *Passion Play* — which happens to end with a Christmas party — is about this paradox. . . .

Anton Rogers . . . plays half of Mr. Whitrow's [James's] consciousness, the half that prompts him in his alibis, watches to see how they are being received, and persuades him to continue the affair. When Miss Whitelaw [Eleanor] has been wised up, she undergoes a similar process of amoebic fission, and acquires Eileen Atkins as a shadow sister, unable to forget and disinclined to forgive.

This is a fruitful but potentially irritating device and Mr. Nichols handles it with great cunning. He refrains from springing it on us until we have become firmly involved with the characters as single persons, and he uses it to show how hopelessly confused they are.

The second act . . . rambles somewhat; but though the play would be neater without it, it would also be poorer. . . .

[James's] attempts to placate [Eleanor] are among the most startling moments in the play. There is in fact quite enough in James to keep two actors employed. . . . The actresses are a little less happy; each has a good scene of desperation . . . but Mr. Nichols seems to be trying with them, instead of being instinctively right, as he is with their spouses.

Mike Ockrent's production — on a split level set by Patrick Robertson with resonances domestic, social, and psychological — is his smoothest to date.

Robert Cushman, *The Observer*, 18 Jan. 1981

It seems to have provoked the most varied reactions . . . from total dismissal to ecstatic praise. . . . Yes, it is true that the second act does not really add to the quite self-contained and self-explanatory first act. . . . Yes, it is true that the main characters are perilously near to stock. . . . Yes, it is true that despite a few desultory crumbs thrown in their direction, feminists have little for their comfort, so maybe Nichols is a closet male chauvinist.

And yet . . . I enjoyed the evening thoroughly and continuously, as much as anything comparable I have seen in the last year. . . .

The idea . . . is that the principals are the present, public person-alities, rather settled, stodgy and middle-aged, while the shadows are different, younger or potential versions of themselves: she independent and trouser-wearing, the raver of her college days with added maturity; he the gleeful overgrown schoolboy buried no doubt in the heart of every prim, menopausal picture-restorer. Nichols must have hit on the idea with his earlier play *Forget-Me-Not Lane*, in the scenes where the grown-ups are on stage with and comment on their tentative teenage selves. . . .

I would have liked to see the device carried a stage further, to include some illumination, or at least validation, of what should be the third principal character, the apparently stupid, apparently sexy girl who makes a habit of stealing other women's safe, middle-aged husbands.

John Russell Taylor, *Drama*,
No. 140 (1981), p. 21-2

On the New York production

The first act, which contains many agreeable turns and twists of plot . . . is so lighthearted that we feel no difficulty in laughing at what is, after all, a classically painful situation. This lightheartedness steadily drains away throughout the second act; we perceive that though the jokes continue the playwright is increasingly in earnest. . . . Nor is Mr. Nichols willing to send us out into the night with merry hearts; confronting us with the possible death of God and the sure old age, impotence, and death of his characters, he ends his play on a note of grim indeterminacy that is likely to set back the cause of adultery by twenty years.

Brendan Gill,
The New Yorker, 23 May 1983, p. 103

The play is clever, impudent, erotic, and an emotional demolition kit.

At his most skilful, Nichols tellingly evokes the Joycean interior monologue in which the tingling shock effect is that of making the holy ritual of the confessional an open secret.

The music of the Dies Irae boomingly punctuates some scenes, and the drama has a neoreligious subtext. James and Eleanor proclaim themselves atheists, but they are wistfully haunted by the death of God.

As this season comes to a close, *Passion* proves to be its most intellectually stimulating and emotionally unsettling offering.

T. E. Kalem,
Time, 30 May 1983, p. 85-6

Poppy

A play in two acts in the form of a musical pantomime, with book and
    lyrics by Nichols and music by Monty Norman.
First production: Royal Shakespeare Company at the Barbican Th.,
    London, 5 Oct. 1982 (dir. Terry Hands; with Tony Church as
    Emperor of China, Jane Carr as Queen Victoria, Stephen Moore as
    Jack Idle, Geraldine Gardner as Dick Whittington, Julia Hills as Sally
    Forth, Geoffrey Hutchings as Lady Dodo, Bernard Lloyd as Obadiah
    Upward, Roger Allam as Lin Tse Tsii, Brian Poyser as Teng Tin
    Chen, Susan Leong as Yo-Yo, Christopher Hurst and Andrew
    Thomas James as Randy, Noelyn George and Sarah Finch as Cherry,
    Jimmy Cassidy, Gary Sharkey, Stewart Mackintosh, and Steve

Simmonds as Clerks, Seeta Indrani as Indian Dancer and Chinese Girl, Michael Gyngell as Tiger, Ken Robertson and David Whitaker as Elephant, Noelyn George as Chinese Dancer, and David Whitaker as Lord Palmerston).

Revival: Half Moon Th., London, Sept. 1988 (dir. Chris Bond; with Josie Lawrence as Dick Whittington, David Ross as Lady Dodo, and Nicky Croyden as Sally Forth).

Published: Methuen, 1982; *Plays: Two.*

The Opium War between Britain and China, which led to the colonizing of Hong Kong Island and the leasing until 1997 of the New Territories, is unfolded, using the popular theatre forms of the musical and the English pantomime. The result is a satire on colonialism.

[Interviewing Stephen Moore, Jack Idle in the RSC production, Sheridan Morley refers to] Peter Nichols's firm statement during the *Poppy* rehearsals that he would never again be writing a play for the British theatre.

Poppy opens tonight at the Barbican, some of its scheduled previews having been cancelled, in a backstage atmosphere of considerable tension: the first new play to have been staged there by the RSC since they arrived in the City last May is a Victorian pantomime of some complexity written by Nichols (with a score by Monty Norman) to tell the essentially serious, ultimately devastating story of the mid-nineteenth century Opium Wars. . . . It uses everything from spectacular transformation scenes to Gilbert-and-Sullivan parodies and, given its essentially Victorian theatricality, the original home for *Poppy* was intended to have been the Theatre Royal, Stratford East.

Then . . . it was taken up by the RSC and assigned to Terry Hands, who early in rehearsal appears to have decided that *Poppy* was not so much a pantomime as a major new musical; at that point the difference with Nichols became most apparent, and at that point Mr. Nichols announced his resignation from the British theatre in a mood of weary irritation.

Sheridan Morley, '*Poppy* in the Wars', *The Times*, 5 Oct. 1982

The arguments between Peter Nichols and Terry Hands over exactly what line the production should take were apparently long and bitter, with Nichols in the end ritually washing his hands of the British theatre altogether. . . . Nichols's original conception of this musical chronicle of the Opium Wars was as a traditional English panto which gradually goes sour. That idea comes over strongly in Terry Hands's production, and it seems fairly immaterial whether the final effect is nearer a Palladium panto or your tattier suburban equivalent. Either way, the audience's responses are guided in a particular direction, which then takes them into a quicksand. . . . Sad that the only person to seem really discontented is Peter Nichols. But at least he has the comfort of being able to cry all the way to the bank.

John Russell Taylor,
Drama, No.147 (Spring 1983), p. 27

It might have been different if the songs had been sung so that the words mattered — or indeed were distinguishable — instead of being belted out like reprises of 'Hello, Dolly'. Nichols may well have a justified grievance against those responsible for the production, who consistently played down the ironies and were evidently determined to create a spectacular show, with all the vigour and vitality of the pantomime and as little as possible of anything else.

Mervyn Jones,
Drama, No. 148 (Summer 1983), p. 8

The fact that [the Opium Wars have] been so neatly erased from the patriotic memory does something to explain why Nichols has decided to tell the story in the ultra-patriotic form of a Christmas panto complete with principal boy, dame, Buttons, and pantomime horses.

Dick . . . loses no time in joining the East India Company and making off to China . . . with most of his old friends . . . and . . . perfectly in keeping with Victorian extravaganza, they encounter the Chinese top brass, embark on brave exploits in remote regions, and finally secure a great British victory; after which Dick returns home to take a golden coach to the Mansion House.

Meanwhile he has turned from a comely principal boy into a hard-faced bully, his beloved Sally has become a dope fiend, and Buttons — alias Jack Idle's old nag — has been shot for horse meat after a farewell song from Jack parodied from 'My Old Dutch'.

That . . . is one example of how the show works. Parody in the early scenes is so much harmless fun. . . . But where, at the start, the audience is asked to give a shout if the two horses get randy, towards the end we are looking out for heads going up on pikes . . . and we are asked to join in a jolly chorus of 'Rat-a-Tat-Tat' commemorating the British sacking of the imperial Summer Palace. . . .

Sheridan Morley has reported a rehearsal disagreement . . . on whether *Poppy* is a pantomime or a musical. The show represents an uneasy compromise.

The production offers a brilliant spectacle; what it sacrifices is Nichols's strategy of beginning from something innocent and familiar and gradually turning it to his own purposes. The show marked a collision beween a writer with a social conscience and a director whose first priority is theatrical effect.

The company, at any rate, have a firm grip of pantomime technique, bubbling over with anti-Barbican gags and joyfully sinking themselves in their well-worn character types.

Irving Wardle,
The Times, 7 Oct. 1982

There comes a glorious moment in Peter Nichols's *Poppy* (Barbican), when Lady Dodo, a pantomime Dame, sings a naughty French chanson called 'Nostalgie de la Boue' to her *déclassé* lover while the pair are followed round the stage by a large white elephant.

At its best the show, a cross between a panto, a musical, and agitprop, is audacious, unpredictable, and wild. But for the most part Nichols's latest (and purported last) edition of his allegories on the state of the nation feels weary and lost within Terry Hands's lavish Broadway-or-bust production. . . .

Nichols sets forth on a fair amount of pedagogy: the second half of the show often looks like the worst of Old Half Moon hectoring, intolerably dressed up . . . and we are told that 'the three C's — Christianity, Commerce, and Civilization' — are a thoroughly reprehensible trinity.

Nichols doesn't make the mistake of turning the Chinese into the goodies, but I could have done with one involving and fleshly hero . . . on which to focus my affections. . . .

He was trying to use this form of popular theatre, which reached its heyday during Victoria's reign, to make a statement about that era. But where is a character on the scale of Aladdin or Cinderella? Where indeed is the story? And why not funny representational backcloths instead of Farrah's exquisitely tasteful flying emblems? And why shroud the live orchestra behind a screen? And do we need the miking?

Victoria Radin, *The Observer*, 10 Oct. 1982

On the revival at the Half Moon Theatre

When the RSC did . . . *Poppy* in 1982, Nichols got so fed up he said he would give up the theatre altogether. Chris Bond's new production at the Half Moon shows that the fault of the original — which transferred to the West End but didn't quite make it to Broadway — was indeed its overblown scale. Nichols had conceived a sympathetically tatty spectacle; at the Half Moon that is exactly what you get. The songs and direct address of panto get across a lot of information, while the comic stereotypes are pure Brecht. Without, of course, anyone noticing the fact. This is good entertainment, but we can also moralize the spectacle. The Half Moon is in the East End, where opium once kept the babies quiet and the sweatshops going. Nicky Croydon's melodramatic decline from principal girl to laudanum addict makes the point. Nichols has sharpened his satire since 1982, for jingoism clearly did not die with the nineteenth century.

Robert Hewison,
Sunday Times, 4 Sept. 1988

A Piece of My Mind

A play in two acts.
First production: Apollo Th., London, 1 April 1987, after touring
  Southampton, Croydon, Brighton, Bath, York, and Richmond (dir.
  Justin Greene; with George Cole as Ted Forrest, Anna Carteret as
  Actress One playing Dinah Forrest, Nancy Fraser, A Marchioness,
  and a Nursing Sister, Jerome Willis as Actor One playing a Critic,
  Charles Upcraft, Walter Forrest, and a Vicar, Gwyneth Strong as
  Actress Two playing Becky Forrest, Upcraft's Secretary, April, Mai,
  June, and an Awards Presenter, and Patrick Pearson as Actor Two
  playing Tom Forrest, an Old Salt, Miles Whittier, Speed, and a
  Hospital Orderly).
Published: Methuen, 1987; French, 1988.

*A playwright, Ted Forrest, has recently died. A critic suggests to
a rival dramatist, Myles Whittier, that Forrest's writing was not
powerful enough to make him survive. Whittier, as a kindness to
the widow, Dinah, decides to write a play in the style of Forrest.
Dinah encourages Whittier to make love to her, partly as an aid*

to inspiration. The ensuing action, set in the dead writer's study, is Whittier's idea of a play by Ted Forrest, in which Forrest is brought back as a character to live again on stage. This device enables Peter Nichols to portray himself satirically as Ted Forrest, satirize rival playwrights, and comment on the art of playwriting.

On a performance at the Theatre Royal, York, prior to the London run

Nichols has a record of turning impossibilities to his advantage: and in this case, he turns the non-event of a writer's block into a multi-dimensional, action-packed comedy, which proves him to still be the grandmaster of stage technique.

The result is a coldly brilliant moral comedy by a man whose profound suspicion of the theatre is the mainspring of his dramatic power.

Irving Wardle, *The Times*, 10 Mar. 1987

On the London production

The good news is that Peter Nichols, five years after renouncing the theatre and all its works, has written his next play. The not quite such good news is that his subject is a playwright who, having renounced the theatre, tries to write novels, finds himself blocked and finally starts his next play. . . . But the even less good news is that in this play . . . the brilliant parts do not fuse into a great whole.

Technically the piece is terrific, it teases expectations and answers them unexpectedly; the ending's double use of double-glazing is as funny and sober a joke as any he has ever given us. But . . . the play is what his pet theatre critic would probably call an interim statement.

Jeremy Kingston,
The Times, 2 Apr. 1987

The cumulative effect is raggedy and painful as the sleeping muse of Ted Forrest, the man whose *Going Dark* won prizes but emptied the stalls, tries everything to kickstart his muse and turn his private life once more to theatrical account. Ted sees himself as a middle-aged man living in a mean time. And unproductiveness is metaphorically aligned with sexual impotency: there is a marked shortage of lead in his pencil.

There are lots of private jokes that sound like revenge and will mean little or nothing to most playgoers.

Michael Coveney,
Financial Times, 2 Apr. 1987

A witheringly funny play about middle-aged failure . . . and combining the virtues of the musical and the confessional with those of a cabaret by Pirandello and a sitcom by Strindberg.

The title holds out promises of arrogance and self-revelation. Both are fulfilled.

Acid and blunt, crusty and proud, Nichols comes across as the Philip Larkin of the theatre. . . . George Cole is irresistible as Forrest: deploying a flawless sense of timing and a gaze which is alternately poisonous and melancholy, he presents an eternal hypochondriac of the spirit, and one of life's masterful losers. This is a comedy written in blood, sweat, and vitriol: I hope the West End is adult enough to enjoy it.

John Peter,
Sunday Times, 5 Apr. 1987

Nichols might well have got away with *A Piece of My Mind* if he'd just carried on fearlessly exploring the meanest, darkest little corners of his soul. But for a writer to insert his own review not only shows he cares more about his reputation than his subject, but it breaks the drama's pace and Nichols's play collapses in terminal self-consciousness.

Mary Harron,
The Observer, 5 Apr. 1987

Indeed it might have been Whittier (or Stoppard) who wrote this play, so cunningly does it juggle with illusion and reality . . . and so brilliantly does it deploy its parodies and word-play. Yet beneath all the artifice, one is aware of a terrible anger, hatred, and sadness.

The anger is that of a man who feels that he has still to receive his due. The hatred is as much for himself for craving that due as for others for withholding it from him. The sadness is for the family which he has slapped about in the act of creation, as the sculptor slaps about his clay. . . . This is a work in which its author seems constantly to be peering, in mingled self-approbation and self-contempt, at his own image in a corridor of mirrors. As one peers over his shoulder, one eventually begins to share his fascination.

Francis King,
Sunday Telegraph, 5 Apr. 1987

You might suspect that both subject and form hold dangers for the playwright. A certain self-consciousness might creep in, especially if the playwright happens to be feeling sorry for himself. Your suspicions would be justified. This is a terribly self-indulgent piece whose whining tone is hardly relieved by feeble humour.

Christopher Edwards,
The Spectator, 11 Apr. 1987

Nichols . . . considers *A Piece of My Mind* to be about other things besides the processes of writing, notably the theme of envy among writers. Abstracting this from the magician's cabinet of the play calls for concentration. The tyranny of form gives us a roughly chronological account of Forrest's career as a playwright, presented as scenes . . . from the work in progress. . . .

Peter Nichols weaves the strands of this breathtaking counterpoint with skill and effrontery, to which the cast of five, playing between them nineteen characters, respond nimbly, with only the occasional grumble about being allowed insufficient time for costume changes.

J. K. L. Walker,
Times Literary Supplement, 17 Apr. 1987

Nichols certainly shows much of his old ingenuity and blithe willingness to play hob with the conventions of formal dramatic construction: in this respect, there are glimpses of the form he showed long ago in *Forget-Me-Not Lane*. His central character and spokesman, Ted Forrest, is in and out of the action as the fancy takes him, sometimes embroiled in events, sometimes addressing us directly. . . . Nichols dredges up his darkest feelings about the insensitivity of producers and agents, even critics, and of course directors.

In-jokes . . . biliously abound, along with much else of interest to no one except, conceivably, other playwrights, many of whom would doubtless enjoy being similarly and bitchily self-indulgent. It is part of the dismaying egotism of the creative life. It may be that plumbers would like to buttonhole us to explain the difficulties they experience in unblocking drains, that dentists would like to elaborate on the intricacies of root-canals and bridgework, but on the whole they recognize that we just prefer them to get on with their jobs.

Next time around, now that he has got this floundering bit of professional exhibitionism out of the way, perhaps Nichols will get on with his.

Kenneth Hurren, *Plays and Players*, June 1987

What attracted George Cole to the play was its pure theatricality. 'It's an audacious piece of work that can only be done in the theatre — and in an intimate theatre like the Apollo. It's not telly and it's certainly not film. Peter just adores the theatre and of course he had to go back to it. You can see in his new play almost a plea for live theatre, which we're always being told is in its death-throes.' Certainly in its obsession with the relationship between life and theatre there are elements in common with *Six Characters in Search of an Author*. . . .

George Cole, interviewed by John Higgins,
'Arthur Daley Going Straight', *The Times*, 25 Mar. 1987

3: Non-Dramatic Writing

Autobiography

Feeling You're Behind. Weidenfeld and Nicolson, 1984;
    Penguin, 1985. [His autobiography to 1971].

In an interview published in *Plays and Players* (June 1984)
Nichols announced his retirement from the theatre. . . . In the
preface to *Feeling You're Behind*, Nichols speaks of his
conversion to prose and reaffirms that his theatrical career is
over. . . . In the early chapters, which deal with the writer's
adolescence in Bristol in the 'thirties and 'forties, there is a
grim, even moving struggle to come to terms with prose.
Handling dialogues seems, ironically, to give Nichols the most
trouble. He is further handicapped by having an irresistibly
quotable father, a naturally theatrical figure who was the
admitted model for the father in *Forget-Me-Not Lane*. After
grammar school came national service, which was a bit anti-
climactic as Nichols turned eighteen in 1946. A constant
theme in the book is that this generation missed a lot of
opportunities, being too young for the war and too old to take
real advantage of the freedom and prosperity of young people
in the 1960s. So the author spent two unproductive years in
India and Malaya, where he proved a very average soldier
and gravitated to the Combined Services Entertainment unit.
Nichols retains the good playwright's chameleon-like ability
to absorb other people's idiom, and the national service
chapter is written as if by a national serviceman. . . . After an
unsuccessful period as an actor, Nichols became a teacher and
married Thelma . . . and they had a severely handicapped
child. The experience took Nichols to the point where the only
way he could deal with his despair was to joke about it, and so
his characteristic style — fusing pain and comedy — was born
in *A Day in the Death of Joe Egg*. . . . As in the play, Nichols
handles this subject with strength and taste, so much so that
audiences and readers may find inspiring what could well have
been distasteful. One opportunity not missed by Nichols is the
one to put the case of the lower middle-class regional Briton, a
case that has been put increasingly over the last thirty years,
but never with more theatricality. It all goes to make a superb
book.

Alexander Buzo, Overland 98 (1985) p. 78-9

What's the matter with Peter Nichols? I mean, why's he so upset? One can understand the tantrums — the exasperation over rehearsals of *Poppy*, leading to the announcement that he would never again write for the theatre. One can understand it as an outburst. What's hard to follow is the repeated airing of grievances — as if the playwright Nichols has had a very raw deal indeed.

Because — and this is the theme of the book, although not a theme which has been properly expressed and explored — he is terribly afraid of having missed out. He should have been to the university (the vivid Malayan chapter is called 'My University'). He should have lost his virginity (and how he goes on about it) much earlier. He should have had much more sex. Up to the age of 40 he was living in 'total obscurity' (yet he was writing television plays). Then he should have become a real writer.

But he is a real writer. What's he going on about?

James Fenton, 'A Book in the Life of a Real Writer',
The Times, 10 May 1984

An unexpected title for a wonderfully funny and courageous auto-biography by a man who has had a string of theatrical successes.

John Mortimer, 'How to Win from Behind',
Sunday Times, 6 May 1984

See also:

Quentin Oates, 'Critics Crowner', *The Bookseller*, 19 May 1984,
p. 2091-93.

Performers give them flesh and a sort of animation, but the real life of a play doesn't start until the public is let in: in other words, when the play becomes interplay. . . . The audience was supposed to be as silent and anonymous as at a Soho strip-club. . . . A less rigid form of this was called naturalism, a purgative reform that became an inflexible genre. A direct appeal, an aside, any breach of the two-way mirror was seen as a sign that the playwright didn't know his job. Yet, of course, there was always interplay: actors responded to the audience, spoke in loud clear voices, waited for laughs, were arranged in pictures that told the story. At its best this fashion made possible the irony and fatalism of Chekhov and Ibsen. We felt powerless to help these poor fools, mirror-images of ourselves, blundering to their doom. The interplay here was odd, tense, as between mortals and impotent gods. We felt for them but could do nothing. . . . No-one pointed out the absurdity of a style that otherwise ignored the audience. . . . It was a form ripe for television and that's what — in the 1950s — it became. The box in the corner is Strindberg's chamber drama, and we can advise and abuse the actors out loud as we never can in the theatre — or cinema. . . . In the course of wondering what was left for theatre to do, I defined a rough approach to playwriting. I would try to find a role for the spectators . . . casting the audience, a method that works best when they're not allowed to settle comfortably into any one role. It's one way of accepting, while at the same time exploiting, the limitations of the form. . . . Inasmuch as I'm thought to have a style at all, it's the use of bits and pieces from the kind of theatre I enjoyed before seeing plays — variety, revue, magic shows, and pantomimes. . . . For many years theatre was the best part of my life. These days I seldom go, not wanting to find myself at some play that pretends to ignore me. 'Communal nonsense' appeals to me more. I enjoy those parts of the event that more fastidious writers find tiresome — the audience assembling, intervals, curtain calls, even the accidents that aren't to do with art or entertainment. I wish I'd seen the performance of *The National Health* when someone in the stalls had a cardiac arrest and, from a stage full of actors robed and masked for a surgical operation, one had to ask, 'Is there a doctor in the house?' The writing of scripts might well go on, even if all the theatres closed, because it is a spare, enjoyable, and demanding form of composition.

'Introduction', *Plays: One*, p. xi-xiv

All the people I write about . . . I take . . . from life. Of course I change them . . . but in fact all my characters are based on identifiable people in life. . . .

I think what a playwright usually does is to respond to something that he can see working on a stage, or on television, or in whatever medium it is that he's writing for. And then after that, as you write it, you write strictly in terms of the individuals. You try not to enlarge it beyond their experience. You try not to make them say things they couldn't possibly say and then you wait for something to emerge out of this.

> Interviewed by Robert McDonald,
> 'An Interview with Peter Nichols',
> *Descant*, Nos. 11-12 (Spring-Summer 1975), p. 6, 8

I always tell young playwrights who ask me for advice that the most difficult thing is to find a director you're close to. . . .

> Interviewed by John Walker,
> 'Meet Peter Nichols',
> *The Observer Magazine*, 20 Feb. 1977, p. 8

My aim is always to be an intelligent entertainer. I believe entertainment is good in itself, anything more is a bonus.

> Interviewed by Jim Hiley, 'Liberating Laughter',
> *Plays and Players*, Mar. 1978, p. 17

I can't write directly about myself — I can only write about aspects of myself put into another character. . . .

The ability to reproduce exactly someone else's tone of voice. It's one of the things I can do. But when the part is given to an actor who can't do that, or who doesn't hear it the way that I hear it, then immediately it's inaccurate.

I've been asking myself the question: if I could write without thinking all the time about the potential effect and appeal of a play, without thinking about all the commercial aspects and all those things you have to think about as a pro, would that mean that I could free myself to start thinking and writing in a new way? Could I retreat from being a very public sort of playwright into something more irresponsible?

Interviewed by Malcolm Hay, 'Piece of My Mind',
Plays and Players, Jan. 1987, p. 4, 5

The whole embarrassment thing is part of the theatre, I think. You know, the idea of trying to embarrass the audience. Anything to prevent them sitting there on their bums having a comfortable time. The thing is to give them an uneasy ride. This is what I think the theatre's about.

I write a lot from notes. I keep a diary and I also keep a lot of notes, so that when I start to write a play I've got certain things that I want to put in, which are like sign posts for the play. . . .

In conversation with Andrew Parkin, May 1987

a: Primary Sources

The Plays

Particulars of individual editions of plays will be found under their respective titles in Section 2. There are also two volumes of collected plays: the first of these exists in two distinct editions, which differ both in content and apparatus, though both go under the same title, *Plays: One*. Earlier references to this volume are therefore followed, where relevant, by the date of the edition, 1987 or 1991.

Plays: One, Methuen, 1987. [Contains *Forget-Me-Not Lane*, *Hearts and Flowers*, *Neither Up Nor Down*, *Chez Nous*, *The Common*, and *Privates on Parade*.]

Plays: One, Methuen, 1991. [Contains *A Day in the Death of Joe Egg*, *The National Health*, *Forget-Me-Not Lane*, *Hearts and Flowers*, and *The Freeway*.]

Plays: Two, Methuen, 1991. [Contains *Chez Nous*, *Privates on Parade*, *Born in the Gardens*, *Passion Play*, and *Poppy*.]

Articles and Essays

'Introduction by the Playwright' [to *Joe Egg*], in Otis Guernsey, ed., *The Best Plays of 1967-68* (New York, 1968).

'Hardy Annual', programme for RSC production of *Poppy*, Sept. 1982. [On pantomime.]

'The Boys in the Black-Booted Ballet', *Sunday Times*, 5 Oct. 1986. [Review article about national service.]

'A Way out of the Dark', *The Times*, 13 June 1987. [On the plight of the West End theatres.]

'A Time for the Children', *The Times*, 26 Dec. 1987. [On Christmas with the family.]

Interviews

Frank Cox, 'Writing for the Stage', *Plays and Players*, XIV, No. 12 (Sept. 1967), p. 40-2.

Vincent Canby, 'Peter Nichols, *Joe Egg* Author, Found Humour in
Desperation', *New York Times*, 3 Feb. 1968, p. 22.

Catherine Stott, 'Plays in the Life of Joe Egg's Dad', *The Guardian*,
26 Jan. 1970, p. 8.

Ronald Hayman, *Playback 2* (London: Davis-Poynter, 1973).

Sheridan Morley, '*The Freeway* and Freedom Going Wrong', *The Times
Saturday Review*, 28 Sept. 1974, p. 11e.

Robert McDonald, 'An Interview with Peter Nichols', *Descant*, Toronto,
Nos. 11-12 (Spring-Summer 1975), p. 5-11.

John Walker, 'Meet Peter Nichols', *Observer Magazine*, 20 Feb. 1977,
p. 7-8.

Jim Hiley, 'Liberating Laughter', *Plays and Players*, Mar. 1978,
p. 14-17.

James Alister, 'All Passion Spent', *Plays and Players*, No. 369 (June
1984), p. 8-9.

John Mortimer, 'How to Win from Behind', *Sunday Times*, 6 May 1984,
p. 9.

Benedict Nightingale, 'The Birth and Slow Acceptance of *Joe Egg*',
New York Times, 24 Mar. 1985, p. 4H.

Malcolm Hay, 'Piece of Mind', *Plays and Players*, No. 400 (Jan. 1987),
p. 4-5.

Nina-Anne Kay, 'Simply a Piece of His Mind', *The Guardian*, 26 Mar.
1987, p. 12.

b: Secondary Sources

Articles and Chapters in Books

Michael Billington, 'Joe Egg's Dad', *The Guardian*, 2 Dec. 1971,
p. 10-11.

George W. Brandt, ed., *British Television Drama* (Cambridge University
Press, 1981).

Enoch Brater, 'Peter Nichols', *The Dictionary of Literary Biography,
Vol. 13: British Dramatists since World War II, Part 2: M-Z*, ed.
Stanley Weintraub (Detroit: Gale, 1982), p. 354-64.

Richard A. Cave, *New British Drama in Performance on the London
Stage, 1970-1985* (Gerrards Cross: Colin Smythe, 1987).

Roger Cornish and Violet Ketels, eds., *Landmarks of Modern British
Drama: the Seventies* (London: Methuen, 1986).

Peter Davison, *Contemporary Drama and the Popular Dramatic
Tradition in England* (London: Macmillan, 1982), p. 115-27. [On
Privates on Parade and *The National Health*.]

Dudley Doust, 'Making Comedy out of a Family Tragedy', *Life*, 24 Nov. 1967, p. 106-9.

Richard Foulkes, 'The Cure is Removal of Guilt: Faith, Fidelity, and Fertility in the Plays of Peter Nichols', *Modern Drama*, XXIX (June 1986), p. 207-15.

Victoria Glendenning, 'Only Four Can Play', *Times Literary Supplement*, 23 Jan. 1981, p. 83.

Ronald Hayman, 'The Mimic Man', *The Times*, 31 Mar. 1971, p. 11.

Henry Hewes, 'The British Bundle', *Saturday Review*, 11 Sept. 1971, p. 20, 54.

Mervyn Jones, 'Nichols', *Contemporary Dramatists*, ed. James Vinson (London: St. James Press, 1973), p. 573-76.

Mervyn Jones, 'Peter Nichols, the Playwright who Has Had Enough', *Drama*, No.148 (Summer 1983), p. 7-8. [Best thumbnail sketch of Nichols's career as playwright from *Joe Egg* to *Poppy*.]

Oleg Kerensky, *The New British Drama* (London: Hamish Hamilton, 1977).

B. Hal May, 'Nichols', *Contemporary Authors, Vol. 104*, ed. Frances C. Lacher (Detroit: Gale, 1982), p. 340-1.

Garry O'Connor, 'Nichols', *Contemporary Drama*, ed. Ruby Cohn, (1982), p. 595-7.

Andrew Parkin, 'Casting the Audience: Theatricality in the Stage Plays of Peter Nichols', *British and Irish Drama since 1960*, ed. James Acheson (London: Macmillan, 1992).

Carol Rosen, *Plays of Impasse* (Princeton, N.J.: Princeton University Press, 1983), p. 25-54. [Concerns *The National Health*.]

June Schlueter, 'Adultery is Next to Godlessness: Dramatic Juxtaposition in Peter Nichols's *Passion Play*', *Modern Drama*, XXIV, No. 4 (Dec. 1981), p. 540-5.

G. W. Stiles, 'Some Thoughts on Two Modern English Comedies', *Unisa English Studies*, No. 9 (Sept. 1971), p. 10-16.

John Russell Taylor, 'British Dramatists: the New Arrivals. No.1, Peter Nichols', *Plays and Players*, April 1970, p. 48-51.

John Russell Taylor, *The Second Wave: British Dramatists for the Seventies* (London: Methuen, 1971), p. 16-35.

Patricia M. Troxel, 'In The Name of Passion: a Comparison of Medieval Passion Plays and Peter Nichols's *Passion Play*', *From the Bard to Broadway*, ed. Karelisa Hartigan (1986), p. 213-22.

John Weightman, 'Metaphysical Voids', *Encounter*, XLIII (Dec. 1974), p. 64-6.

Albert Wertheim, 'The Modern British Homecoming Play', *Comparative Drama*, No.19 (Summer 1985), p. 151-65.

W. B. Worthen, 'Deciphering the British Pantomime: *Poppy* and the Rhetoric of Political Theater', *Genre*, No.19 (1986), p. 173-91.

Reference Sources

London Theatre Record, 1971, bi-monthly, in progress. [Reprints reviews from all major newspapers.]

Kimball King, *Twenty Modern British Playwrights: a Bibliography, 1956-1976* (New York: Garland, 1977), p. 69-75.

Carolyn Riley and Phyllis Carmel Mendelson, eds., *Contemporary Literary Criticism, 5* (Detroit: Gale,1976), p. 305-9. [Reprints extracts from reviews.]